Getting off the Merry-Go-Round

*How to Create the Life You Want
Without the Fear, Doubt and Guilt*

Jan Janzen

Women Empowering Women Inc.

*Getting off the Merry-Go-Round: How to Create
the Life You Want Without the Fear, Doubt and Guilt*

Printed in Canada

Library and Archives Canada Cataloguing in Publication

Janzen, Jan, 1961-
        Getting off the merry-go-round : how to create the life you want
        without the fear, doubt and guilt / Jan Janzen ; Dale McGowan, editor ;
        Chris Price, illustrator.

        1. Self-actualization (Psychology) in women. 2. Women–Psychology.
        3. Women–Conduct of life. I. McGowan, Dale II. Women Empowering
        Women Inc. III. Title.

HQ1221.J358 2008   158.1082   C2008-905026-6

Dedication

Since the day you came into my life Greg, your reassuring presence has been a solid and trusted rock. Your belief in me has been unwavering and your unconditional love a blessing. Thank you for being such a gift in my life.

Monique, your firm but loving guidance has been a beacon of light. You are an amazing vehicle for Universal wisdom. Thank you for being such a wonderful guide and trusted friend.

You are both a constant source of encouragement and inspiration for me to continue growing. I am so blessed to be in your lives daily, no matter where I am in the world; to feel your love and trust your support. Thank you for being who you are and allowing me to fully be who I am. I love you both very, very much.

Acknowledgments

Someone asked me the other day how many people are involved in publishing a book. There are many people who are hands-on in the process and many who inspire and cheer from the background. I quite simply work with the best of the best—people who love what they do and it shows.

Dale McGowan is a great editor to work with. He is honest, open and on time—qualities that rank very high on my priority list. Thanks Dale for another wonderful job and for the encouragement and support for what you called a "fascinating project."

I would write books just to work with my formatter, Diane Mendez. Diane is deaf, which I learned after she worked on my first book. Her beautiful gifts of encouragement and being in service are so clearly evident by her enthusiasm, creativity and her passion for making a book look terrific. Thank you, thank you Diane for a stunning job! I hope you know from my emails how loved and appreciated you are.

Chris Price is a jolly North Carolina man who has worked with me on a number of projects. He made me laugh every morning as he sent me the morning comics—my illustrations. Chris is dedicated, easy to work with and fun. Thank you Chris for a fabulous book cover and absolutely amazing illustrations.

Karen Learmonth is my wonderful photographer who creates magic behind the camera. It's an absolute delight to experience her creativity and brilliance while she makes me feel extraordinarily special. Thank you Karen!

I want to thank all of my incredible clients who gave me permission to use their stories, although the names have been changed to protect their privacy. It's a very personal experience to be "in session" with me, so I appreciate their willingness to share with others the learning we both received from the Universe.

And to all the clients whose stories were never written about in detail in the book, your courage to grow and be everything you are meant to be has certainly been a huge encouragement to me over the years. I have learned so much through you. Thank you for stepping up to the plate. You are honored, valued and loved for who you are.

Thanks to my great friend and mentor, Peter Comrie, for being there for me, for being the sounding board, the firm voice of guidance, the reality check. But most of all, thank you for always believing in my potential.

Thank you to my great friends, Jnana, Bobbie, Josette, Kelly and Brenda, who always show up at the right time with a word of encouragement, a bit of much needed advice or a hug. Your presence in my life is much appreciated, valued and honored.

To my dear sister Julie who loves me unconditionally and shares my passion for personal freedom. Your constant help in the practical areas of my life allow me to do what I do as I live out of three suitcases galavanting around the world.

I am very blessed to work with some very powerful angels in the work I do. I never feel alone but always feel guided in bringing the wisdom from above to a situation. It's a very beautiful and peaceful feeling. Thank you to my heavenly partners.

And lastly, to my best friend and partner, God, who guides me every day. We have a pretty radical relationship but it works, and I love it. I just knew when to sit down and write this book and then I was literally given the words. Thank you, God. We make a great team!

Jan

Foreword...

This journey called life can be rocky. With unsure footing, we muster our courage and take our forward steps, like children finding our way. Some steps are taken alone, some with others. There are steps that are easy when our way is clear, and these are blessings. But there are also times when we lose our way, find ourselves misguided, and backslide. All our work, our tenacious forward movement, feels like little more than futile baby steps.

Then, in my experience, angels appear. They are in human form, but of course they would be. That seems to be how it works here. Like energetic bridges, they point you gently back onto your path, which was not a Grand Canyon leap away after all. You just lost your way. They gently remind you of who you are and guide you to reconnect to what really matters.

Jan Janzen is one of those angels. In her book *Getting off the Merry-Go-Round: How to Create the Life You Want Without the Fear, Doubt and Guilt*, she blesses you with heartfelt wisdom to help you get unstuck, to help you remember the special spirit which lives in every part of you.

I have studied and read countless experts in my 25 years of private practice, and Jan Janzen is at the top of the list. She clears the way because she is a clear teacher. She is gifted, compassionate, and gets to the bottom line quickly and efficiently.

Jan's story is so inspiring. Through her spiritual search and communication with the powers that be, she has been given an amazing gift of hearing, knowing and healing that places her among the *crème de la crème* of therapists. Her many years of working with people and the outstanding results they experience give hope for those who feel lost and stuck.

Jan has a sixth sense, a special connection to people that helps facilitate permanent and lasting change. Her story reminds people that they have the same resources available to them. Her own challenging background combined with her God-given gifts enables her to work with chronic and difficult behavioral patterns. When she looks into her client's souls, the results are nothing short of spectacular and amazing. She sees what most cannot; she shifts what feels immovable.

What Jan has to offer the world is a rare and innovative technique. She teaches you how to reconnect with the deepest part of yourself and most importantly to remember who you are and how important your destiny is. That's what *Getting Off the Merry-Go-Round* is about. Be prepared for some eye-opening concepts as Jan writes about everyday problems in an innovative and life-changing way.

I don't read many self-help books any more as they are all the same stuff in some homogenized form. But this book is different. Don't expect to read what you already know. I read every page from top to bottom. It touched many deep places in me and presented me with some new thoughts and a better understanding of myself.

There are so many delightful insights in store for you in this book. You will love hearing about your five CEOs—an easy to understand, clear and concise explanation of who you are. I LOVED learning about sacred gifts. This chapter alone will free you from guilt and allow you to focus on what matters. Jan's understanding of the importance of prenatal work and its value is often overlooked but Jan explains it so simply. You will let go of so much guilt just by understanding the impact of this special time in the womb. I LOVED the concept of 'courting peace as your lover.' WOW—genius and powerful! She also presents a completely different insight into 'procrastination'—another powerful concept to eliminate guilt and help one to focus.

What Jan writes about money will give you the courage to change. She spells it out so people can grasp what is truly possible.

Getting off the Merry-Go-Round presents practical information you can begin using immediately to make your necessary changes. The book reflects the tremendous insight of the author and also the knowing that the Universe expresses through enlightened humans. It will thrill your soul. Jan's truly amazing gift of vision and understanding grants you permission to be all that you ever dared to dream you'd be. After reading these inspired pages, you will shift. Your core will be changed for the better, forever.

Catherine Cardinal, Ph.D., author of
A Cure for the Common Life:
The Cardinal Rules of Self-Esteem

Introduction...

Imagine you are six years old again. You're at the playground. The monkey bars, the teeter-totter, the swing set, and the merry-go-round all beckon as you run from one to another. The monkey bars are a bit scary as you hang upside down. You push hard on the teeter-totter so you can "bump" your partner. You ask for extra pushes on the swing, soaring so high your stomach jumps.

At last you head for the merry-go-round. You run and push the bar to get it going as fast as you can before you jump on and enjoy the ride. You feel the wind in your hair, the thrill as a friend gets it going even faster and jumps on. You hang on with both hands as you go around and around.

Now you want to get off, but the merry-go-round isn't slowing down. More and more people are coming on, each pushing it harder and faster. They're pushing you as well, and you're now in the center. It's very crowded on your merry-go-round. It's not fun anymore. You're tired. You're hungry. You want it to stop but it won't. No one is listening as you plead for it to stop. No one is even paying any attention to you. It just keeps going round and round and round. You feel sick, scared and angry. You're stuck, trapped. It's out of control. *Is anybody listening? Does anybody care? What am I going to do?* you wonder.

I remember many days feeling like I was on a merry-go-round and just wanting it to stop. Perhaps you can relate. You know that feeling of spinning so furiously in circles that you feel dizzy, out of control, and a bit sick. That feeling that you just want everything to stop for a day or a week so you can catch up and rest.

Would you like to get off the merry-go-round? How do you make the dizzying merry-go-round of life slow down? Can you actually get off, or has it all become too complicated? Is it even possible to stop it now that so many more people are on it with you, depending on you to keep it going? The reassuring answer is yes, yes, yes. You can stop it. This book will tell you how.

Jan

Chapter One...

Rudy walked into the condo a few minutes before 5:00 p.m. I was getting ready to pack up for the day. The moving sale had been a moderate success, but the living room was still amply stocked with goods that needed to be sold. As he got closer, I took another look. The man standing in my living room looked just like Dustin Hoffman.

As Rudy bent to examine some items on the floor, he asked me, "So why are you selling everything?" I replied, "I'm moving to Mexico and I need to get rid of it all." He was quiet, but a moroseness enveloped him like a swaddling blanket. He spent an inordinate amount of time examining each object as if he wanted time to stand still. The thought went through my head, "God, I hope he's not a rapist or psycho." The realization that I was all alone in my apartment with a strange man suddenly seemed obviously dangerous.

Rudy collected his small pile of things and we negotiated his bill of $12.00. I asked him if there was anything else he was looking for. From his position on the floor, he looked up at me with a wistfulness in his eyes and said nothing.

Then it hit me. "You want to do what I'm doing, don't you?" I asked. His eyes turned into pools of dark emotion, and he simply said, "Yes."

"So why don't you?"

Rudy told me the all-too-familiar tale of why he couldn't do what he really wanted to do. As a music teacher with a family to support, he had obligations, a mortgage, and a daughter who might require some medical attention. He had a job, a commute, a life that he hated. It was sucking the life out of him. He knew that, but he didn't know how to stop the blood from draining. He needed a tourniquet and a blood transfusion but didn't even know how to ask. He just stared at the open wound of hating his life and felt hopeless and helpless at what he saw.

In a span of thirty minutes, I learned that Rudy wanted to move to a tropical place. He wanted freedom, he wanted to spend time with his precious family, he wanted to have a life but he was scared to death. He had even been offered a teaching position in the Bahamas, but the lack of job security terrified him. He had turned it down because of all the unanswered questions. What about the medical situation for his family, the instability? What would happen after the three-month trial period? He listed all the reasons why he couldn't just pack up and go.

"Rudy, you are dying. Your soul is dying. I can feel it. I know it. You can feel it. You know it. You have to start listening. This is not going to go away. It is not going to get any easier. Your soul needs to go and you know that. I strongly suggest you do something sooner rather than later." I spoke frankly with him, feeling his pain and knowing he was like a terminally ill man, his hope for life draining with every step he took.

He nodded his head, afraid to speak, and quietly left with his $12 worth of goods. Rudy didn't need a new hammer or a hot plate for his wife. Rudy needed a new life.

     Getting Off the Merry-Go-Round

Chapter Two...

The morning sun shone brightly through the window. The noise of the ocean, the same dull roar that had lulled me to sleep last night was now gently bringing me back to the day. I lay there for a few minutes, fully grasping the reality of the moment. It wasn't raining. It wasn't even gray. The sky was a brilliant robin egg blue. I smiled. How could I not? I was exactly where I wanted to be—in Mexico in a beachfront condo—and this was home for the next several months. I smiled even more.

The mango was so sweet and juicy, I ate it with my fingers for the sheer delight of being able to. My scrambled eggs had tasted even more delicious this morning, even though they had been my regular breakfast for as long as I could remember. This morning there was a special richness about them. Maybe it was because I ate them outside, even though it was the end of January. As I plopped another cube of randomly cut mango into my mouth, I watched the men fishing in the early morning hours, patiently waiting for the fish to bite. They had not a care in the world, and neither did I.

I closed my eyes and smiled. And my mind drifted back to a time a few years ago that was not so sweet or carefree—when it was tears, not mango juice, pouring down my face.

Chapter Three...

"I don't want to be married to you anymore."

"You what?" I barely uttered.

"I don't want to be married to you anymore," he repeated, clearly relieved that the words were finally out of his mouth. I stared at him aghast. In the pit of my stomach, I knew he was telling me the truth, a truth I never thought I would hear. Although my gut knew it to be the truth, my head was still reeling. I looked at him through the spinning vortex of all the implications of those words sinking into my head. How can you be married to someone for 18 years, know every intimacy with this person, then in a nanosecond feel like you are staring at a complete stranger?

Two and a half months later, Stephen moved out. It was Labor Day weekend, 2000, and it was the closest I had come to labor. The tears had flowed like Niagara Falls. The pleading, the anger, the guilt, the sadness, the grief. It felt like every emotion had enjoyed its season, sometimes simultaneously. My heart had been ripped out, cut up and handed back to me in pieces. In the short period of twelve months, just one year, everything I had known and loved was gone.

Stephen and I had chosen to leave our religion of upbringing the previous September. Having both been raised as Jehovah's Witnesses, we decided to move on and out. It was a challenging decision as the concept of excommunication is real and alive with the Witnesses. With that decision, we lost our families, our friends and every bit of structure we had ever known. Suddenly Saturday mornings were ours for the first time in our lives. No more banging on doors, peddling *Watchtowers* and *Awakes*. No more Bible readings to do, daily texts to study, no more meetings to attend and prepare for. We were free!

While we felt free, it felt very strange. I looked at the NO BLOOD card I had carried in my wallet for over twenty-five years, a legal document stating that I would rather die than take a blood transfusion. I put it back in my wallet where it stayed for another two years before I felt ready to part with it. Christmas that year was quiet. We had no idea how to celebrate it and no new friends to celebrate it with. On the other hand, it was a relief to start believing that the end of the world was no longer imminent as it had been for our entire lives.

As we moved into the new millennium, we felt excited by our future, stimulated by the decisions we faced and challenged in our relationship. We had been through challenges before—this was no different. Or so I thought. And then the day arrived when Stephen said, "I don't want to be married to you anymore." That was the day my world came to an end. My personal Armaggedon had suddenly arrived.

Chapter Four...

Within 24 months of Stephen moving out, I went from being happily married, earning a six-figure income, and living in a beautiful home overlooking the ocean on Vancouver Island, to being divorced, on the verge of bankruptcy and homeless. My mother had told me before I got married that you never knew a man until you slept with him. Pretty useless advice for a young Jehovah's Witness woman committed to virginity until her wedding night. But it didn't matter anyways because Mom was wrong. The truth is that you don't know a man until you divorce him.

Divorce, no matter how civil, is never pleasant. I had watched my parents divorce after 47 years of marriage; and as they divided the salt and pepper shakers, as in "Ruth, you take the salt and I'll take the pepper," I knew I would never go down that same path. Stephen left me with all the worldly belongings and I wrote him a check that would supposedly tide him over until he could get his life together.

It didn't work that way. In very little time, two sensible, hard-working people with perfect credit ratings, who together had always been financially responsible, were now in the depths of financial despair—and we had managed to create the chaos completely independent of each other. It was amazing how the tables turned from prosperity to poverty virtually overnight. I now knew what it was like to walk into a store and wonder if my credit card purchase would go through. I soon learned what it was like to have those credit cards taken from me personally.

Yet in those 24 months, I had walked on fire and jumped off of cliffs, suffered through a sweat lodge and broke arrows with my throat. I had done everything I had been told was necessary to get my life back on track, yet had gone from bad to worse. My leg in a cast with torn ligaments, my last major account cancelled, I hit rock bottom. While

I was living with a friend in one room, trying to stave off creditors, my perfect credit rating down the toilet, Stephen phoned one night and asked if I would pay for half of the reversal of his vasectomy so he could have a child with his soon-to-be wife.

Between my laughter and my tears, I felt every bit of anger at my life welling up in me. He really couldn't be serious!

But he was. In 1991, we had sold everything we owned and moved to Ecuador to serve as missionaries with the Jehovah's Witnesses. Not sure about the birth control situation in that country, we had opted for a vasectomy, a decision Stephen paid dearly for. Now 10 years later, he was asking me to share in the expense of having it reversed. Barely making my rent payment and my car lease, I felt like every decision I had ever made in my life was now in my face, sitting there like a big fat ugly pimple at the end of my nose. I never felt more like a failure than I did in that moment. It was surreal. Could I really be in this big of a mess? My creditors confirmed I was indeed in serious trouble. Now Stephen was remarrying and asking me to help pay for an operation for a woman I didn't even want to know about. I was all alone, definitely broke and more than hurting. It was a major wake-up call.

Chapter Five...

I got on with my life. After Stephen left, I moved in with a boyfriend and tried to build businesses and a networking organization to raise money for charity. I had minor successes but certainly not what I expected.

Nothing was smooth. My new relationship was challenging. My business in the automotive industry was getting harder and harder and the annual event for charity I was organizing was taking up too much time with no financial rewards. I was becoming more and more bitter, resentful and angry. I deserved so much more than living in an ugly apartment with a man I no longer wanted to be with, struggling to pay the bills, and afraid to move out on my own.

When I finally did have the courage to leave, I had no idea the worst was yet to come. It did go from bad to worse. I moved into a room in a friend's apartment, which she used as an office, and I was literally kicked out of my home each day until her clients would leave. There were many nights when I had to be out until late at night while she finished her appointments. I would sit in my car outside the apartment, unable to enter my own home. I hated the situation with every fiber of my being but felt hopeless and helpless to change it.

Faced with bankruptcy, I had to make financial choices that allowed me to pay back part of the debt but would leave my credit rating in shambles for years. It seemed like every forward step I managed to take, I took three more steps backward.

It was then I began to re-examine not just the surface of my life, but the deeper choices I had made. When I left the Jehovah's Witnesses, I had thrown the baby out with the bathwater. Disillusioned with major religions, I was adamant that I wanted nothing at all to do with God. My motto was, "I don't do the G word."

It was in the midst of the anguish of being alone, broke, homeless, angry and sick, that I felt the twinge to return to God resurface. At first it felt strange, but slowly it began to feel more familiar.

One night in a fit of tears, desperation and terror, I flung myself on the bed and prayed for the first time in years. It was a prayer of anger, a prayer of despair and a prayer of absolute surrender. I was exhausted. Worn out, broken, destitute and humble, I talked to God and begged for help. I had been taught to pray since I was a little child, but this was no "Our Father" that I prayed that night. I'm sure I made the angels blush!

Shortly thereafter, I noticed an ad in the local paper for some personal development lecture at a place called The Center for Positive Living. I had no idea it was an actual religion, but I liked what I heard about the Law of Attraction and Spiritual Mind Treatment, a positive form of prayer. I began to re-examine my spirituality with a whole new twist.

I signed up for courses and began minister's training. Every extra penny I had, and even some that weren't extra, went into my courses. Those courses challenged me, provoked me, and forced me to look at many of the disempowering beliefs I had been raised with that were still hanging onto me like barnacles to a ship.

My faith in God was renewed and invigorated, even as it went through a major overhaul. A Bible scripture I had been raised on— "Happy are those conscious of their spiritual need"[1]—went through my head constantly, and I realized that no matter what our spiritual beliefs are, they are intrinsically wound up in our happiness. Whether spirituality meant walking in the woods, working with the homeless, meditating or knocking on doors offering Bible education, every person was conscious of a deep spiritual need within. I felt the chains of long-held beliefs, the need to be right, the fear of doing wrong, the guilt of past actions, and the constant expectation that something bad

---

[1] Mt 5:3 ("Blessed are the poor in spirit") as it appears in the New World Translation favored by the Jehovah's Witnesses.

was about to happen. All these and my tendency to berate myself for not being good enough—something that had been indoctrinated into me as a child—were now obvious to me. I had previously just accepted all this as a way of life that was expected and normal. Now at least I saw the chains, but they were persistent, numerous and strong.

Over the next two years, life began to come together again in a new and positive way. It certainly wasn't any overnight success. I moved to an apartment I could afford in a suburb of Vancouver that was right in the midst of drug dealers and prostitutes. As I put the pieces of my life together, police raided the neighbors for drugs, and mice invaded the apartment building. I worked at my business with a mouse trap of sticky paper and peanut butter at my feet and hookers walking the street. But at least it was a place to call my own. At least I could go home when I wanted to. I relished that small piece of freedom that I no longer took for granted.

Like a pit bull with lockjaw, I pursued more answers than my minister could provide. I wanted results and I wanted them quickly. Nothing seemed fast enough as I sped through the courses in record time, wrote my minister's exam and came out at the top of the class—only to realize that I didn't want to be a minister associated with a denomination. That would limit my access to answers, I decided— answers that I was still fighting for daily. I read books, attended workshops, and listened attentively to the information that was finally starting to come in. I had argued with the Universe, beseeched, pleaded, and threatened God with an urgency that was almost hysterical.

I was possessed by a need to know why, despite all the personal development work, all the spiritual training I had done, my life wasn't working. I was still broke, my two best friends had abandoned me on the same day, I was still restless inside at a core level and my career was unfulfilling, stressful and financially challenging.

Yet people talking to me would listen in disbelief at the chaos in my life. It was obvious to them that I wasn't stupid, lazy or incompetent.

"Why is your life such a mess?" they would ask incredulously. One well-meaning friend said, "Jan, the outer chaos is a reflection of the chaos within." I looked at her with tears in my eyes, knowing that she had no idea how chaotic I felt at a soul level. Topsy-turvy, upside down, backwards and inside out was how I described my emotions, beliefs, and thoughts. There was nothing peaceful, calm, or serene about what was going on inside and showing up in my life. Looking back now, I realize that despite my belief that nothing was changing, I was knocking down walls of negative programming and years of emotional abuse. I'd had a difficult start; my mother had been addicted to Valium, smoked and drank, when she unexpectedly got pregnant with me at 39.

Told I would be Mongoloid because of her advanced age, my parents had fought violently during those months as they were making the challenging transition to becoming Jehovah's Witnesses. Going from a life of smoking, drinking and adultery to get on the narrow road the Jehovah's Witnesses demanded was anything but easy.

Added to all of that early emotional trauma for me was 38 years of being raised in a very strong religious cult. I never thought I would get to school because the end of the world was coming. I then never thought I would graduate, marry or see 40 because Armageddon was always imminent. And add to that almost 20 years of marriage to a husband who was a controlling perfectionist and triggered my fear of men.

I didn't appreciate how much I was going to have to change to come to a place of peace, calm and serenity. Overnight miracles were happening, but I sure wasn't seeing them. I just felt driven like a sailor in a storm, looking for calm waters.

Like many on the personal development journey, I felt angry. I wasn't sitting around twiddling my thumbs and contemplating my navel, after all. I was working hard at this journey, but I didn't appear to be getting much right. I was willing to do whatever it took—and my bank account proved it.

I had been down this road a decade earlier when I was physically ill returning home from Ecuador. Suicidal, depressed, with virtually no immune system, my husband and I had spent thousands and thousands of dollars looking for a solution to get me well. I was going weeks without sleep and was so exhausted I had given up driving and even using a knife in the kitchen. I'll never forget when someone said, in a very patronizing tone, "You don't die from insomnia."

"YOU will," I thought, "when I bloody well kill you!"

Those were not good days. Exhausted because he wasn't sleeping well due to my horrible insomnia, Stephen started giving up. At one point someone suggested taking algae. He passed the suggestion on to me but said he didn't think I would be interested. I looked at him outraged and said, "Stephen, I would stand on my head and stick cucumbers up my nose if I thought I would get well"—a saying I now use often to indicate that I will do whatever it takes to get a job done. It must be the visual on that one that somehow resonates. But Stephen got the point—we were NOT giving up as long as we had a dollar in the bank and I had a breath of life in me.

We bought the algae. One year later I was dancing through my days in amazing health. So I wasn't going to give up easily on the personal journey either, but as I looked around, I certainly wasn't impressed with the overall results. For all the hundreds of millions of dollars spent on personal development, there were still a lot of good people with pretty messed up lives, and I was right up there at the top of the class for failure. But I remembered my persistence with physical challenges and kept on searching, asking and demanding.

Finally, finally, finally, amongst the mice and the hookers, my fervent prayers started to be answered. My life started changing. Bit by bit, slowly but surely, it transformed before my eyes. Although the changes were a combination of many things—and for every person, every workshop, every book and certainly every friend who contributed to these changes I am truly grateful—the greatest changes came from information I learned straight from the Universe, from God. I spent literally thousands of hours "in the lab" with God. What

I was taught brought me from homeless and destitute, unhappy and desperate, to living an amazing life on the beaches of Mexico, a life that is peaceful, calm and serene, exciting, fulfilling, and truly joyful. Would you like to know what changed me from bitch to healer, from broke to abundant, from fear-ridden to peaceful? In the pages of this book, I will share with you everything I learned. Is it for real? You bet it is. Countless clients have now worked with me and achieved amazing successes of their own. You really will understand, for the first time, how to get off the merry-go-round of insanity and create the life of your dreams without the fear, doubt, and guilt. This is not your typical, create-a-vision-board, affirm-your-intention-and-monitor-your-thoughts solution. I promise. What I will share with you may rock your beliefs, shake your core and stretch your comfort zone. When you think I'm crazy, really off my rocker, remember that I was once homeless and broke and I now live in a beachfront condo in Mexico. This is the truth with a capital "T" as my dearest friend Monique calls it. It really is this simple….and it really is this complex.

Chapter Six...

As God will come up a lot in this book, perhaps we should start with that subject. Despite being raised with a very black-and-white view of God, let me assure you I am now about as gray in my viewpoint as a Vancouver sky in December. I couldn't care less if you believe in God or not. I don't care if God is Jehovah to you, Buddha, Jesus, Mohammad or a walk in the park. It doesn't matter one iota if your God is saving a tree, a hot bath by candlelight or a Catholic Mass on Sunday, complete with confession. I did enough judging about that subject in 38 years to last many lifetimes. It simply doesn't matter. I don't think God really cares either, because we are probably all so far off-base regarding what God is that God probably gets a good chuckle out of it all.

What I do believe is that there is some Higher Power, a Source of all life, and that this Universal Spirit appears to know more than anyone I know. I mean, who else could create a baboon with a bright red ass and a beautiful rose with the same color? I'm impressed with that level of imagination and creativity. You have to be pretty amazing to have done everything I see around me, so whoever did all that, for me, is God. You can call "It" whatever you want. I will refer to God as "him" only for the sake of convenience, as I can't really imagine that God is anatomically correct. My only issue with the word "It" is that it sounds more like a neutered pet rather than the most incredible power in the Universe. So in this book, I will just call "It" God because that feels best for me. I've tried the rest on for size, and I come back to God every time, so I'm sticking with the title, but you can call God whatever you want.

That we even believe other people should think the same way about God as we do simply amazes me. How would any woman feel if she walked into a party and everyone was wearing the same dress? She'd be pretty miffed and would probably want to leave the party immediately. How would any man feel if he drove the same car as every other person in town? The pain would go far beyond the frustration of trying to find your car in the shopping mall parking lot. Our choice of car is about our personal identity at a much deeper level. We identify ourselves by our clothes, our home, our hairstyle and our car. We don't think everybody should do everything our way in any of those areas. Why would we expect the entire world to think the same way about God as we do?

What I am very clear about is that the character behind that title of God has changed dramatically—from angry, jealous, vindictive and demanding to loving, peaceful and supportive. I much prefer the God I love today to the God I grew up with. So did God himself change? I doubt it—but my views on God have certainly done a 180-degree turnaround. So now that we've got that out of the way, let's get on with what God told me as I pestered and amused him with all my questions.

Chapter Seven...

So what exactly does "being in the lab with God" look like?

First of all, God does not wear a white coat and sit at a microscope with a Petri dish. Some of the details are now sketchy because I tried a lot of things to get answers out of the Universe (although for better or worse, I never did stand on my head and stick cucumbers up my nose), but it went something like this. I would ask a question. I would then either wait for an answer to come into my head or use a pendulum, my body as a pendulum, or whatever I had handy to get a "reading." I would ask really specific questions, such as, "So what does the Subconscious Mind do, other than look after body functions? Does it look after emotions? Yes. Good, what emotions?"—and the answers would come in.

I would then take those answers and start experimenting on myself. One night, after doing some weird and wonderful experiment, I felt this incredibly strong sensation, like a slipped bicycle chain suddenly falling back into place on the teeth of the sprocket. The sensation started in my toes and went straight to my head, ending with a BANG!

I felt a bit stunned and had what I affectionately referred to as one of my "H.S." moments—which does not, by the way, stand for "Holy Spirit." The impact was so strong that I really wondered if I had done some serious damage.

The next morning all seemed well. By the end of the week I had dissected what had happened. I then started experimenting on friends —helping them make the same little shifts I had accomplished in my life. When the fifth one in a row told me she felt exactly the same feeling of lightness, happiness and clarity, I was dancing on the ceiling. You'd think I had just discovered a million dollars!

I continued asking, investigating, and drilling God and myself for the answers. Finally I am sure that God just figured, "Tell her what she needs to know, will you? She deserves to know." I felt like Jacob in the Bible who wrestled with an angel all night, despite his hip joint being out of place, just to get a blessing. Finally at dawn, the angel blessed him and Jacob was satisfied. His name was changed to Israel and he went on to become father to the nation of Israel.

I too was wrestling with God and getting my blessing, but it was coming in bits and pieces, dribs and drabs. Then one day, Carol, one of my business coaching clients, was struggling with this really annoying cough that just wouldn't go away. Out of my mouth came these words, "why don't I do to you what I do to myself?"

I suddenly recoiled. "Oh my God," I thought. "What will my clients think if they see the weird work I do on myself?" Obviously this was a belief that wasn't very positive, but all I remember is that she said, "Yes."

Carol started coming to my condo for her appointment every week. She sat on my couch and we started digging in her for answers just like I had dug in myself for my own answers. Carol started to have some breakthroughs. I offered what I was doing to more clients and started doing it on the phone. I worked with more and more clients and now have done well over a thousand healing sessions with people all over the world, getting amazing revelations and answers. Once I started sharing the gift and the knowledge with others, it seemed as if the information came in by the truckload. And the more information I got, the more questions I had. God and I were full-fledged partners by now. I was renewed and excited to take my life to new levels.

Have I learned it all? I certainly hope not. But what I have learned has transformed the lives of hundreds of clients. They have seen remarkable shifts in their way of living, a deeper peace, a greater sense of joy and a remarkable understanding and appreciation of who they are. Some families have been brought together; other families have been able to separate in peace. Weight has been lost, sex lives have improved, bank accounts have grown, ailments have disappeared, children have changed, grades at school have improved, bad habits have vanished, careers have blossomed, and self-esteem has sky-rocketed.

I don't have a degree in biology or psychology. I haven't taken any healing courses like Reiki or done anything scholarly to get the level of understanding that I have. As a matter of fact, I nearly failed Grade 10 science. But I find it interesting that when a medical doctor consulted with me about a patient of his, I described to him what looked like frayed electrical wires that had been stripped of their plastic coating and explained to him exactly what effect this distraught nervous system was having on the person.

He said, amazingly, "You're seeing the myelin sheath!" I had never heard of any myelin sheath before—I have since learned it is an insulating layer around neurons, just like the plastic coating on a wire—but he, thank God, understood exactly what needed to be done to solve the problem based on my description.

Another example: I always saw cells spinning, oftentimes erratically. It was only about a year ago that I learned from reading a biology book that cells do indeed spin along with their DNA.

I was also told in one of my sessions with God that I could talk to cells—a practice you will learn for yourself. It's a very effective way to create lasting change. I have spent many a day talking to liver cells, heart cells, and systems in the body, not knowing that a healer by the name of Julie Motz (author of *Healing Hands*) goes into operating rooms and talks to organs as they are transplanted from one patient to another. It was fascinating to read her experiences, as I understood exactly what she was doing and could have answered some of her questions about how to work more effectively with the organs.

Just recently I received a newsletter reporting on scientists in Russia who have discovered ways to communicate with DNA and get it to change. The parts of the DNA they thought were "junk" are actually highly communicative parts of the cell. These scientists now realize you can affect DNA through ordinary language and frequencies! I didn't realize these were all new revelations in the arena of science. And for my naiveté and ignorance on these matters, I am truly grateful. I took the insights I was given and ran with them, not knowing they weren't the common belief or had not yet been discovered within the scientific community. I trusted God was telling me the truth, and I just tried to be the best receiver of information that I could be. We seemed to have made a very good team. Equally important, God gave all of this information to me using examples and metaphors that are easy to understand. I guess he remembered I had almost failed Grade 10 science.

Chapter Eight...

Imagine a company with five CEOs. Every morning they stand in front of five different elevators in the same office building and wait to go to their separate offices on separate floors. They never talk to each other, yet at the end of the month, their bankbooks are expected to balance with each other. Impossible, you say—and you are absolutely right.

Imagine a company in which only two of the five CEOs ever attend meetings, receive memorandums, or are consulted about how to run the company. How successful would that company be? Not very. Yet these two scenarios describe exactly what is happening in your life.

What if you were made up of five CEOs? Let's think of it this way. Your conscious mind—the one that nags you, hounds you, natters at you all the time—is one of your CEOs. Though it really shouldn't be, it's the one that is probably in charge of your life. Your conscious mind operates completely from a place of fear and doubt, fueled by the "what-if's" of your life: What if it doesn't work? What if it does? What if I quit my job—how will I pay the bills? What will my friends say? And on and on and on. It never seems to stop, the mental diarrhea. We need some Imodium, and fast! Although your conscious mind is absolutely essential, it is far too fanatical about knowing all the answers immediately. There is no place for faith or trust. As for patience—now you're really asking for miracles. Your conscious mind just needs to know what to do next, what's coming, what's happening, and what's going on, so it can worry, ask more questions and keep you on that merry-go-round of fear and overwhelm.

Sound familiar?

T. Harv Eker of Peak Potential Training fame, one of my first mentors in the personal development industry, calls it "mind frick." It's a more polite way of expressing something much stronger, something that affects everyone, including the leaders and trainers of the world. Buddhists call it "monkey mind," this constant background conversation going on in our heads. Would you be surprised to learn that I have very little monkey mind? I do not have a mind that chatters, nags, or operates from a place of fear.

I recently heard someone say the only way to overcome the monkey chatter of negativity is to drown it out with the positive. In other words, play the opposite even louder. I disagree. Come to understand why your conscious mind is freaked out, worried and nagging, and then direct it to stay busy doing what it loves to do and does well—and the mind chatter goes away. Otherwise, it is no different than a parent wailing louder than a screaming kid! However, find out why the kid is screaming, alleviate that problem, and you won't have to shout, wail or holler. What a relief! You'll learn in chapter 75 how to work with your conscious mind in a way that truly alleviates mind frick. It's quite amazing to live with a peaceful, organized, and helpful conscious mind, rather than with the pandemonium of fear and overwhelm.

Now let's meet another of your CEOs—the Subconscious Mind. Like a giant storehouse, your Subconscious Mind files every single word, every single memory and every single thought you have had—ever. So what would you be thinking about if your car was stolen, your dog got run over and your kid's teeth got knocked out today in a fight? Would you be thinking about the great eggs you had for breakfast, the smooth trip in to work, or the sunny day? Probably not. Instead, you would most likely spend hours, days, weeks, months and even years talking about your car being stolen, your dog dying and your challenging kid.

The Subconscious Mind says, "Wow, this must be important. She's been talking about this for days. We need to place this one right at the front of the file so we can access it constantly." So every time you park your car in an underground parking lot like the one where your car got stolen, your Subconscious Mind reminds you that your car was stolen there, and you feel uneasy.

Isn't it also interesting how bad things seem to repeat themselves in your life? Those negative situations get filed with little red flags that say to the Subconscious Mind, "This is important." Your Subconscious Mind is amazing. It works to keep everything running in your body automatically, and thank goodness for that.

Your conscious mind would really be freaking out if it had to look after all of that, in addition to its own workload. But an important thing to know about the Subconscious Mind is that for every file, there is an emotion. You simply can't remove the file without removing the emotion attached to it. Why not? Because it is the emotion that gives the file a negative or positive charge. Otherwise the file is simply a word, an action, a thought or a response. You may think of eating a steak dinner as romantic, healthy, wealthy, or desirable. A vegetarian may think of eating that same steak dinner as barbaric, disgusting, cruel, and undesirable. Do you see how the file of eating a steak dinner can have very different emotions attached to it? The same thing happens with EVERY single file. So the emotions linked to the files are critical and are creating the results in your life more than you realize. We'll be talking a lot more about this in further chapters, because once you understand this, you've got a massive part of the solution understood.

There are three other CEOs. You rarely hear about them, so prepare to be surprised.

Chapter Nine...

The third CEO is your body. The body has an abdominal brain, which Edgar Cayce, writing in the early 20th century, called more powerful than the cerebral brain. Yet nobody even talks about it today.

In the pit of your stomach, housed in the solar plexus, is a brain that is connected to your digestive system and other vital organs. It's why you get a "gut feeling" or feel "sick to your stomach" when an emotion is triggered. Your abdominal brain houses all of your emotions. Edgar Cayce was absolutely right—your emotions rule your life, not your intellect.

I live on the seventh floor of a condo overlooking the Pacific Ocean. I love watching people approach the edge of the balcony and hang back, afraid they will fall over. Seriously, unless someone pushes you over the railing or you stand on my patio table and jump, it is physically impossible to fall over the edge of the balcony. Yet people hang back all the time, afraid they will fall. Is that your cerebral brain or your abdominal brain? It's your abdominal brain. Your cerebral brain logically knows you cannot fall. Your abdominal brain, armed with the emotion of fear, has come right to the forefront and will stop you from leaning over the edge to get a good view.

The abdominal brain is not just worried about heights. So how else is it stopping you in your life? It controls your finances, your work, your relationships, your sex life, and just about everything else you can imagine. You are run by emotions in that abdominal brain and I bet you never even knew it existed. If an abdominal brain is running my life, I sure want to know about it, how to communicate with it, and how to get it to cut me some slack in every area of my life.

This isn't about falling off a balcony, or not. This is about creating the life you say you want.

Ever wondered why you can't get off the merry-go-round of dieting, illness and exhaustion? Does it sometimes feel like your body is your worst enemy as you drag it around like a weighted anchor, hoping it will cooperate and get you through the day? You can get some remarkable shifts in perspective when you learn how to deal with the third CEO, an important member of your team.

Chapter Ten...

Spirit is another CEO. This is not exclusively religious; every major philosophy in the world acknowledges that we have some sort of life force active within us. That energy, breath of life, Qi, Holy Spirit or spirit is also your unique life force, and it is powerful. It's the same force that moves the oceans, keeps the sun, moon and stars in alignment, and creates tsunamis and hurricanes. That is the power you have access to.

Yet most people's lives reflect anything but power. What happened? Think of a water hose attached to a tap. You can have the tap turned on fully, but if the hose is kinked, knotted or twisted, the water will not flow through the hose. What prevents Spirit from flowing fully through your life? Emotional issues, past and present, belief systems that don't serve you, genetic coding based in scarcity, fear and lack, and tribal mentality beliefs you have absorbed automatically. Start to release those emotional issues and Spirit will flow through you more powerfully.

If you took a cup of water from the Pacific Ocean to a laboratory, that water would have all the qualities of the Pacific Ocean. Pour it back into the ocean and it will be re-absorbed. You could never take out the same cupful again, ever. Likewise, we get our "cup of Spirit" when we come into the world, and when we take our last breath, it goes back into the Universal Ocean of Spirit.

But in the meantime...

In the meantime, we have access to very powerful energy. It has all the qualities of that Universal Ocean of Spirit, which is pretty impressive if you believe that this Spirit created everything we see. Spirit also has qualities which are essential to a productive and powerful life, and when those qualities are missing in your life, you suffer from a "broken" Spirit. Love, joy, peace, goodness, kindness, and compassion are just a few of those qualities. Joy is critical to Spirit and the precursors to joy are fun, laughter and play. When was the last time you humored your Spirit and had some fun, laughed 'til your belly hurt, or took some time off to play? If you've got a grumpy Spirit, it may be that this CEO is telling you something. Start appreciating how amazing the very life force is that you breathe in and out each and every day, and you will walk a little taller.

Theoretically we should be able to walk on water and raise the dead. My attitude is: It's okay if I don't, but I'll take everything short of that, thank you very much!

Chapter Eleven...

The fifth CEO is your soul. Again, this is not an exclusively religious concept. In my experience, we have given very little thought as to why we are here. Why did your soul choose to be on this planet in the 21st century? Having been given the gift of being able to communicate with people's souls, I was stunned to find out that not every one of them is a happy camper. Not everybody came to make the world a better place. Many souls are discontented, pissed off and disillusioned with their choices for this lifetime. Until you deal with your soul and its purpose, I assure you, your life will never flow smoothly.

Your conscious mind should not be in charge of your life, but it probably is. If you don't think it is, who is worrying you and stressing you constantly throughout the day? It really is your conscious mind. If Bill Gates offered to run your company instead of some twenty-year-old high school drop-out, would you take him up on it? Put your soul in charge of your life instead of your conscious mind, and your life will dramatically change.

Lastly, once you realize that every thought, action, and situation that has ever occurred to you in this lifetime or in any past lives—and yes, I believe you have had many—is recorded in your Subconscious Mind, that will explain most clearly why your life isn't working in certain areas.

Negative experiences carry a very high charge because we give them the most energy. Remember the car being stolen, the dog dying, and the kid's teeth being knocked out in a fight? The problems will be the first and predominant part of your conversation. Just ask someone how their day is and you will generally hear the negative first. Listen to yourself and you will hear that firsthand. Unfortunately, the negative will take priority and will get the more prominent file in the subconscious. Thereafter, the subconscious simply pulls the most prominent file—why wouldn't it? Nobody has ever directed it to delete all of those files, complete with all of their emotional counterparts, from this life and all past lives at a DNA and cellular level, and pull only positive files. Well I did and you can. It's not that hard—you just have to know how.

Working with all five of your CEO's—conscious mind, Subconscious Mind, body, spirit and soul—will change your life, just as it would change a company's success. You can go from disaster to diva, from broke to bountiful, from helpless to happy. There is no stopping your success once you understand how to work with your five CEOs. You've got a team to work with, and I bet they're great.

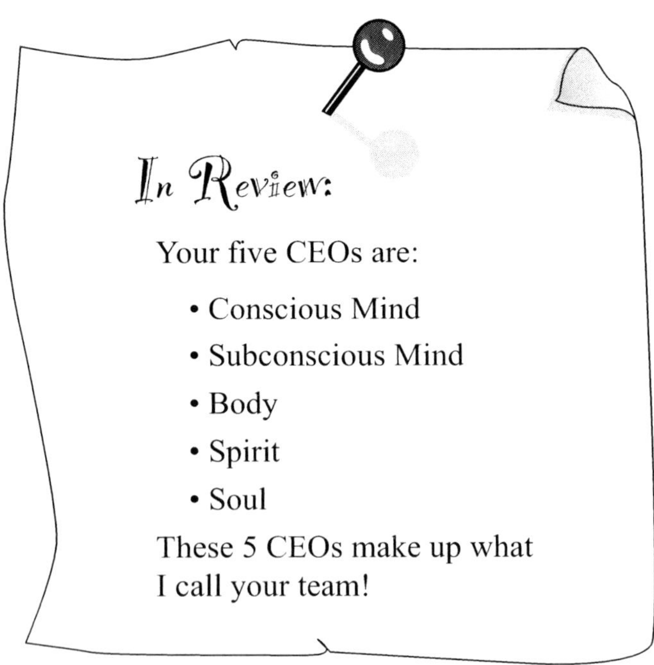

Chapter Twelve...

Most people will agree that emotions play a large part in their life. They also often feel out of control when it comes to handling emotions, as those emotions can be overwhelming and dominating. The majority of people feel that fear is a big part of their problem—fear of success, fear of failure, and fear of rejection, to name just a few. Although we have come to dread the emotion of fear, fear is actually an important part of our psyche. We need fear to survive, and as every one of your CEOs is predominately concerned with safety and survival, trying to eliminate fear completely is like wrestling with a python. In later chapters, however, I will deal with the issue of fear.

I believe that anger is actually far more damaging in your life and pervades every area of your life, including anger towards parents, marriage mates and partners, children, God or some Universal Power and yourself. Start to eliminate that anger and that kinked, knotted, twisted hose will begin to smooth out.

Start to look at where you are angry. If you're still talking about something your parents did to you when you were five, you're still angry. If you can't attract a mate into your life, then you're angry at the sex you are trying to attract. You may be angry around sex as there may have been abuse during childhood. Get out of the box with this one and start writing down everyone and everything you're angry at. The list may be long, but until you have released anger, you will never have peace, joy, love and prosperity in your life. Guaranteed.

One of my clients argued with me that she wasn't angry at God. Viewing herself as a very evolved, spiritual being, this idea was almost repugnant to her. Yet in a healing session with me, I could see her as a little girl, sitting in church with her parents, watching the collection plate being passed. She was angry that she had been told there was no money for something she wanted earlier that week, yet now there was money for God. The moment I told my client what I saw, she burst out in anger and said, "I wasn't two or three. I was about five and I was pissed off. I remember that now!" I suspect that five years of age was the first time she remembers it consciously—it was not the first time it occurred. We healed the anger, and her business increased, her personality softened and her health improved.

How do you release any emotion? Emotions need to be released at a DNA and cellular level— otherwise, they just get moved around and are never fully released. I spend hours a day talking to people's cells with dramatic results. Cells carry what best could be described as a backpack of garbage. Eventually, when the cell gets too overloaded, it can't do its work of defending or repairing your body, or reproducing healthy cells, which is when disease sets in. When you let go of the backpacks of negative emotions and beliefs, the cells literally lighten up and you feel noticeably lighter.

A conversation with your cells sounds something like this: "I release at a DNA and cellular level, all anger around my inability to carry through an idea, all anger around my laziness, all anger around my fear from both this life and all past lives. I release all anger around my insecurity about whether I am good enough, my anger at all past failures, my anger that I gave up too early, didn't follow through, didn't persevere and was afraid."

Once you feel complete in releasing the negative, then you can move into what you do want your cells to resonate. "I KNOW in every cell of my body, that I forgive myself for everything I have done in this life and all past lives. I know in the DNA of my cells that I am good enough, that I am powerful, that I am amazing, and that I am fully and completely capable of doing what needs to be done to bring incredible success in my life." This is just an example. Every one sounds very different. As there is release, you may feel it, but you will also feel where there is tension, and that is where there is still a blocked emotion or belief. You'll feel like a combination of detective and attorney, as you negotiate your way through the files of beliefs and emotions that are making up your life.

You can do this with every emotion—fear, depression, despair, sadness, guilt, anger, unworthiness, hatred, grief, powerlessness, worry, doubt, frustration, etc. You can also release at a DNA and cellular level any and all beliefs that are not serving you.

Does this take some work? You bet. Cleaning out your garage, your filing cabinet or your closet takes some work too. Isn't it worth it to have a life that is peaceful, joyful, prosperous and loving? If you are thinking it's too much work, then that's the very first belief to release. "I release at a DNA and cellular level the belief that I am not worthy of being a success, that having what I want in life is too much work, that I don't have the time, the energy, nor the resources to let go of my disempowering beliefs and create an amazing life. I let this go in this life and all past lives. And I KNOW that I am worthy of success, I deserve to be prosperous, abundant, peaceful and joyful. I am powerful and I KNOW that I can be anything and do anything—I have the power." Try this yourself. You may feel a little silly at first, but go lock yourself in the bathroom if you need to and talk to your cells. They'd love to have a chat. Seriously!

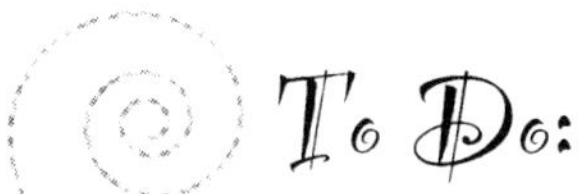

To Do:

Relax: I have a bonus gift just for you at www.anamazinglifenow.com that will help you to start working with yourself. The first word of Chapter 31 is the password.

Chapter Thirteen...

Did you start to do some clearing? I hope so. I continue to clean on a regular basis. Whenever an emotion comes up that leaves me feeling anything but peaceful, joyful, prosperous, or loving, I start releasing until I feel the joy and peace come back into my life. Five minutes or less, and I am back on track. With a bit of practice, you can do the same.

What makes this different from other techniques, like reciting affirmations? Sometimes you get lucky and hit on the right affirmation to bring about a bit of a shift; but more often, people get frustrated repeating a mantra that doesn't appear to be doing anything. Suppose you want more money in your life. So your affirmation is, "I am wealthy, abundant and prosperous in all areas of my life." A month later, you're still not wealthy, and the affirmation is in the garbage bin.

Perhaps "wealthy" has a negative file linked to it that is very overbearing. Perhaps your programming as a child, your genetic coding, or a past life experience around wealth was violent, abusive, or frightening. Perhaps your grandparents had been wealthy but were specifically targeted during the First World War, because of their wealth or business success, and lost everything. So what ended up in your "wealth" file? *Being wealthy is dangerous. You don't get to keep your wealth. Your loved ones are attacked when you are wealthy.* Any one of these or a combination could be in that file. Your five CEOs (who only have your safety and survival at heart, remember) will look at that file and say, "No way. We are not going down that path. It's too dangerous to be wealthy"—and they simply won't create it.

People whose ancestors are from Eastern Europe or Scotland and Ireland have very strong subconscious files that wealth means being lorded over or being the hated one, and that wealth is only for the aristocracy. Consequently, any affirmations around wealth will bring up subconscious files that resonate with those beliefs, and wealth will be elusive and evasive.

Many people think their beliefs and emotions are filed away neatly, as if California Closet has been through, sorting them all nicely into individual folders. Not so! Beliefs and emotions look more like dog food that has gone through the blender. I don't tell you this to discourage you—only to help you appreciate why you may not have had the outstanding results in your life that you desired. Treatments, healings, courses, workshops, affirmations, books, CDs, and meditations may have all helped to some degree, but until you work at a cellular and DNA level and work with **all five** of your CEOs, you will always have limited success.

How do I know that? I have worked with millionaires and multi-millionaires who are outrageously successful. Yet, many areas of their lives are a mess. Physically and emotionally, their relationships and their stress levels are in crisis. They are working hard to hold on to their success and are afraid they will lose it. I don't know about you, but I knew I wanted my success to look entirely different from that.

Clear the negative files around wealth and find an affirmation that resonates with your cells and you will see success. But I firmly believe that once the cell gets the correct message, affirmations become a moot point.

An example. I was a slob for most of my life. Didn't make my bed, didn't hang up clothes, didn't put the dirty dishes in the dishwasher and never organized my office. Files were everywhere, never mind finding two shoes that matched or my car keys. Now I could have done affirmations 'til the cows came home, telling myself that I was a neat and tidy person, and it wouldn't have made one iota of difference. Believe me, everyone tried. Spankings, embarrassment, threats by my parents, even a fanatically tidy husband, all failed to change me. Nothing did for 43 years!

However, once I cleared the beliefs and emotions around being tidy, I woke up and automatically made my bed. I found myself automatically putting the dishes in the dishwasher. If I turned to walk out of the kitchen without putting them away, I found myself turning around as if something was wrong—and I'd walk back and put them away. I even automatically hung up my clothes. Once the cells are back on track, it happens automatically. If it doesn't, that's the big clue that there is still a belief or emotion around this area of your life that hasn't been resolved. Resolve it and let the problem solve itself automatically.

I know that disorganization is a big issue, so here's a related story. After listening to me speak about my healing work and hearing this story of never making my bed, a woman came up to me and confessed that she too was a slob! She put things in corners and consequently found herself surrounded by piles of clothes, books, and anything else that would fit into a corner. I identified that she had a boundary issue—she was essentially marking her territory, much like a dog pees on trees and bushes to mark his territory.

We healed her need for the boundaries, and the next day, she was so excited to share with me that when she went to put something in the corner, she literally stopped midway there and completely changed her mind *automatically*. Then when she couldn't find something that morning—it wasn't in any corner—she realized she had actually put it away—*automatically*.

You're a complex human being. There is nothing simple about you. You are a fascinating combination of beliefs, tribal mentality thinking, past life experiences and genetic coding. Let's take a look at one area in particular to see just how complex and fascinating you really are.

Chapter Fourteen...

Every one of us has inherited specific traits or genetic coding from our ancestors. Interestingly, in working with people from all over the world, I have found that certain genetic coding is very predominant in various cultures. For example, working with an African-American person, fear of being controlled, fear of stepping out and speaking up, and a feeling of inferiority will show up every time. They also carry a tremendous amount of pain from slavery, as well as a fear and distrust of authority.

Someone from Eastern Europe will have a belief that life is hard, that something bad will happen, that war will break out, that depression, economic hardship, famine, epidemics, and sickness are normal, and that death is always imminent. Life is a difficult struggle. A person from Scotland or Ireland will feel very differently about their posture in life compared to someone from England, where the genetic coding is about supremacy, conquering, and superiority—although it's all done in a very genteel, aristocratic style.

Genetic coding, inherited through our DNA from our parents, has a tremendous effect on your life. I recently worked with a client with genetic coding from the Ukraine. Now an older woman, Maria was amazed how the belief systems about what "a good Ukrainian woman" should do for the men of the household was now playing out in her life as she cared for a 90-year-old mother. Her beliefs about responsibility, and even her feeling that her brother should be excused from sharing in the care of their mother, was weighing heavily on her.

Your genetic coding can have a tremendous effect on you, from your weight issues to your bank account. There are lots of programs in our genetic coding that are really powerful, such as the ability to work hard, think fast on your feet, strive for excellence, and be a good cook.

How exactly does this affect what you get in life? Again, your Subconscious Mind will pull the most dominant file around every single thought you have. If famine, starvation or cruel slavery are an integral part of your genetic coding, then an overriding belief that something bad will happen will lead to you playing it safe, staying small, or never really exerting yourself. Let's face it—if you had been whipped, flogged or raped by a harsh slave owner, it makes sense that your files around men would not be all that positive.

One of my former clients is Chinese. When in a session I brought up her Chinese genetic coding, her immediate reply was: "I don't even think of myself as being Chinese." She didn't see that her genetic coding had anything to do with her failure as an entrepreneur. However, after clearing the beliefs around business and entrepreneurship that were part of the genetic coding of the Chinese, her business literally turned around in days. Today, more than 18 months later, her business is flourishing.

We all have different ways of responding to our genetic coding. I personally made soup. My two freezers were full of soup. Every free moment I had on the weekend, I made soup. I would open my freezer, see all the soup stored in it, and feel safe and secure. One day I realized I didn't care what my savings account looked like, how much money I had to my name, or how many investments I had. I felt safe because I had soup in the freezer. Absolutely crazy but true!

So what's my genetic coding, you ask? My father was born in Russia. What does a good Russian woman always have on the stove? Good soup. The ruble may plummet, war may come, the government may be overthrown, but a bowl of soup—now that fixes everything! I released those beliefs and lost the fervent, panicky, obsessive need to make soup. It took me seven months of eating soup daily to go through all of my soup. What was fascinating was that as my soup stock dwindled, my bank account soared. So don't laugh when I say that your food habits alone may well illustrate what beliefs are running your life. But there are more reasons why you do what you do.

          Getting Off the Merry-Go-Round

Chapter Fifteen...

What is Tribal Mentality? Tribal Mentality describes the set of beliefs that you have picked up from the Tribe. If, for example, you were walking through a room filled with smoke, could you avoid breathing in smoke? Obviously not. Well, today the world is full of what Richard Dawkins first described as memes—ideas that are repeated and passed on until they are believed and accepted by the masses. Most of these memes or Tribal Mentality beliefs are absolutely false, but as Lenin stated, "A lie told often enough becomes the truth."

There are millions of Tribal Mentality beliefs about money that you have picked up just by virtue of walking through this world with all of its propaganda and programming around money. "Money is hard to get." "Money is hard to keep." "Rich people are evil." "Rich bitch." "Dirty money." "If I'm rich, everyone will take advantage of me." These are just a few of the millions of Tribal Mentality beliefs or memes that you have picked up. For every time you say you want more money in your life, I bet there will be a Tribal Mentality belief that deflects it or offsets it.

Tribal Mentality beliefs are insidious. There are so many of these beliefs that we just accept because they are part of our inheritance from the Tribe. In North America, we accept that menopause entails a wide range of health issues that require "fixing" or dealing with at some level. Go to Africa and you'll find an entirely different perspective on menopause—that of a woman moving into the most respected and wise years of her life. So a Tribal Mentality belief is simply a belief that we accept as true, proven or not. But the more people that believe it, of course, the greater the power the belief has—and it can become "true" by virtue of the power we give it.

We are not independent thinkers to the degree we like to suppose. Becoming aware of Tribal Mentality beliefs is quite fascinating as they affect every single aspect of our life, from religion to media to authority to sex to how we dress. Remember that your five CEOs are predominately concerned about safety and security, and remaining a part of the Tribe has traditionally been critical to safety and security. As a result, you tend to cling to the tribal beliefs whether or not you consciously believe them.

The rules and regulations of the Tribe currently control nearly every aspect of our lives. Try going through the airport security without complying with the rules of the Tribe! But it is actually far more pervasive than that. We'll be looking at many Tribal Mentality beliefs throughout the book. By now, I hope you're starting to understand that who you are is complex and amazing, while recognizing that so much of what you do is more on autopilot than an expression of conscious choice. But by releasing old beliefs and becoming more of a witness to your own actions, you can change that, recognizing they are, for the most part, the result of beliefs you don't even agree with.

Chapter Sixteen...

So how does an understanding of your five CEOs, of Tribal Mentality, of Genetic Coding and of how your cells work affect you getting off of the merry-go-round? You may not want to live in Mexico like I currently do. Or maybe you do. You may not want to do major philanthropic work or quit your job. Or maybe you do. But whatever your goals and dreams, you probably feel stressed. You feel, "If the world would just stop for a day or two, maybe a week or two, I could relax and get something done." You're too busy. You've got too much on your plate. Your daytimer is overloaded and you feel overwhelmed, stressed out and guilty about everything you haven't got done. As we go through and talk about everything from weight to sex, Mom and Dad to religion, this life and past lives, you will come to understand how all of these have contributed to the crazy-busy, never-truly-satisfied, itching-to-be-more-than-you-are kind of life.

But there's a place to start to recreate your life with peace, joy, love and prosperity, and that is with the simple word NO.

We're actually going to set some boundaries for you. Perhaps you have never been allowed to set boundaries without feeling guilty. Maybe you learned that the word NO wasn't allowed. You are going to learn to say NO without the guilt, the fear and the doubt that the world will fall apart when you set boundaries.

What is so difficult about the word NO? Does it make you feel like you are a failure because you can't do it all yourself? Let go of that belief at a DNA and cellular level. Does the word NO make you feel guilty because you have been taught that you should always be nice, kind, spiritual and giving? Well I have news for you—it's the word YES, not NO, that makes you less nice and less kind.

Saying yes all the time builds resentment and anger inside of you, which produces some pretty nasty side-effects—snapping your kids heads off, yelling at your spouse, hating your boss, and cutting off the person behind you on the freeway. The built-up resentment from saying yes all the time makes you a bitch, and yes, men can be bitchy too. You feel overwhelmed, stressed out and anything but nice, kind, spiritual and giving. Just watch yourself for a day or two and see how often you react out of anger and resentment. No, you may not be throwing frozen dinners across the kitchen at your husband, but you may not have had sex with him in months. No, you may not be beating your kids, but you may be shutting them in a room for hours with a video game, movie or computer and thanking God for the distraction that is giving you some peace and quiet.

When you wake up with a cold, the flu or a sore throat and can't go to work, you may be happy that you just get to stay in bed for the day and do nothing except finally look after yourself.

    Getting Off the Merry-Go-Round

I don't know these things for sure, but I know you do. You know exactly how you are demonstrating your anger and resentment at always being at everybody's beck and call. Who says you have to answer the phone every time it rings? Last time I checked, that wasn't part of the phone contract. There are answering machines for a reason —let them do their job. Who says emails have to be answered within 24 hours or you're a worthless business person? Since when does agreeing to be on every committee, fundraiser and field trip make you a better parent? It's simply not so….unless of course you have been programmed to believe that it is, and then nothing in the world can change that except you. So let go of the belief, at a DNA and cellular level, that you have to be perfect, everything to everybody, always available, constantly at your family's, bosses' and friends' disposal and that you cannot say NO without feeling guilty. Let go of the anger and the resentment that you have not set boundaries, that you have not taken time for yourself, and that you have the belief that saying NO means no one will like you.

Ouch, that one hurt. We'll talk about that next, but right now you need to start saying NO. Practice in the mirror, practice with friends, practice a scene in the car and say NO until you can say NO without the guilt. I live by a motto that "NO is a complete sentence." It doesn't mean I don't sometimes explain myself, but it does mean I don't feel obligated to do so out of guilt. Sometimes the answer is simply NO, and I prefer not to go into an explanation. But right now, simply get comfortable with NO, a little word that will change your life.

Chapter Seventeen...

We have this program and belief that everyone must like us. It's simply not true—in fact, it can never be true. Will everyone ever really like you? No, they won't. Do you like everyone? Probably not. So why would everyone like you?

In my first book, *Devil with a Briefcase, 101 Success Secrets for the Spiritual Entrepreneur*, I devoted a chapter to this very subject. It is so important to let this one go. Just think about this—there has never been a person in human history who was universally liked. There are people who don't like the current President of the United States, who don't like Oprah Winfrey. I am sure many people thought Princess Diana was just a walking fashion plate, and Mother Teresa apparently had a strong tongue that didn't always go over so well. I doubt everyone will like you either.

So let that belief go at a DNA and cellular level. That's a biggie. If you try to please all the people all the time in your life, you will end up on that merry-go-round of "I hope I am good enough for you" nonsense, which is a losing battle. Acknowledge right now that not everybody likes you, you don't like everybody, people will not like some of your beliefs and that's all okay.

The one person who does need to like you is you. If you don't like yourself, then you are in for big problems, something you probably are already well aware of.

We have been programmed through our genetic coding that we need everyone to like us because otherwise we will not survive. Really? That may have been true in small communities where we needed our neighbors to help us build our barns, birth our babies and help us through crisis, but your survival is no longer dependent on whether or not the entire world likes you. It's really not. Your DNA is still very much programmed for that small community thinking and it needs to change. You like yourself, and that can change everything. I learned this through many examples in my life.

In 2004 I was running a very successful women's organization in Vancouver. Sold-out workshops and an annual event to raise money for charity were the mainstay of my business. Suddenly I decided to go volunteer for eight weeks in South Africa. I put the business on hold, never to return to doing monthly workshops. The organization folded later that year and I proceeded with my life.

Did some people not like that decision? You bet! They loved the organization and the handholding that had been provided for them in growing their business. They had their opinion of what I did, and it wasn't necessarily favorable. Others celebrated my courage to pick up and go to a foreign country, noted for its dangers, and follow my heart. Some liked it, some didn't—a pretty typical response from what I've seen.

When I returned that fall and started the first home pole dancing company, the you-know-what really hit the fan. As a newly ordained minister, a so-called "respectable woman," and a business leader in the community, what was I doing swinging around a stripper pole (regardless of the fact that I was fully clothed)? Some people were outraged, some spoke very badly of me—and others couldn't wait to attend or host the first party.

So when I talk about this subject, I speak about it from a lifetime of experience. Going from door to door as a Jehovah's Witness, with a very hard-hitting message of doom and gloom, was anything but popular. I've been mobbed, had dogs sicced on me, hoses turned on me, and many a door slammed in my face. I can honestly tell you that the opinion of others is far less important than whether YOU like you.

Religious programming is an especially potent source of this need to please everybody. Fail to please everyone and you are wicked, selfish, evil and all sorts of other not-so-nice names. Jesus didn't please everyone and they crucified him. Neither Mahatma Gandhi nor

Martin Luther King, Jr. pleased everyone—they were both assassinated. These were all deeply spiritual men, clearly anointed to do a significant work on this planet, and they weren't welcomed with open arms, accepted by all, and loved by the masses.

So are you ready to let go of that belief that everyone needs to approve of you and speak well of you? Good, because letting go of that one belief will make a world of difference in your life.

To Do:

Start by looking at one area in your life (eg. money, sex, relationship, career, health, energy) and write down your beliefs around it. A big clue about what your beliefs are in this area is what you say about it.

Here's an example: **You lack energy in your day.** Do you say things like: I am just getting older. I have a lot of stress in my life. I don't get enough sleep. I am always tired. There's just too much to do.

These will ALL contribute to your team doing exactly what you believe, think about, and talk about!

Chapter Eighteen...

How are you doing? I have probably hit some big beliefs in your life, so take a deep breath and let's continue.

What do you want in your life? Do you really know? Have you been too afraid to find out? Sometimes that subject can feel more like an irritation than anything. "Why does everybody keep on asking me what I want?" you may be screaming. "I DON'T KNOW!"

You do know what you want, but most likely you stopped listening to that voice so long ago that it is now a whisper. I remember teaching a workshop in Calgary about finding your passion. A woman in the audience said her passion was buried so deeply she would need months to find it. I invited her to the front of the room. Within 90 seconds, she told me what she would love to do in her life. She was so convinced her passion was buried that she didn't even realize she knew it. Once she was given permission to just say what she wanted, out it came! This is important. You do know at some level why you are here. But unfortunately, many people believe it's ridiculous to think they can do what they want.

Two things are happening in this case:

1. Sometime between being in utero and five years of age you got put into safe mode.

2. You have been programmed to believe that you can't have what you want.

So what does it mean to be put into "safe mode"? When you turn on your computer and a virus is attacking it, what does it ask you? "Do you want to boot up in safe mode?" Something similar happened to you. Perhaps life in utero wasn't so wonderful. Maybe Mom didn't want you. Maybe Dad didn't want you. Perhaps Mom was ill, over-whelmed by older siblings, or exhausted physically because of pregnancies that happened too closely. Perhaps they were both worried about the financial repercussions of having another child. You know exactly what was discussed and thought during those nine months in utero. Many clients I have now worked with have realized how traumatic those nine months were in their life before they even physically entered the world.

Scientists are now beginning to realize that every emotion that Mom felt, you felt. As an empath, I feel many different sensations while in a healing session. I feel pain, burning eyes, nausea, terror and a host of other delightful emotions and reactions as I work with my clients. One of the strangest reactions was a choking sensation. It felt like a piece of black pepper had become lodged in my throat. I started coughing and was very uncomfortable. Realizing this was my client's reaction and not mine as I dealt with her challenges in utero, I immediately asked if her mother had smoked during pregnancy. "Yes" she replied. I instantly saw the visual of my client as a fetus grasping the umbilical cord as she tried to stop the toxins from entering her body. As she did that, she of course cut off food supply and oxygen, but she was concerned about the toxins more than food or air. Now she was overweight and didn't understand why she couldn't get off the merry-go-round of obesity, the feeling that she needed to fill her face, almost in a panic, as if the food supply was going to be cut off at any moment. She was put into safe mode while still in utero, and nobody had ever told her cells and DNA that she could stop worrying about not getting enough food, or that she no longer had to fear for her food supply and could eat more normally.

Another client, born in Eastern Europe, had severe emotional issues because she had shut down her feelings. She would say to me repeatedly, "I just don't feel any emotion." In working with her and taking her back to utero, I learned that Mom had already had several abortions. Due to a change in government policy, the abortion planned for my client was delayed several months and eventually never happened due to the delays. Imagine being in that uterus and feeling all of the emotions from Mom about you being killed. Imagine being in a uterus that had already experienced several abortions and was now anticipating another one. She wondered why she struggled with her emotional void. It soon became obvious that she had been put in safe mode while still in utero.

Childhood abuse, whether physical, emotional, sexual or spiritual, is a common reason we shut down. We determine fairly quickly that this world isn't safe and we need to do whatever it takes to survive. Once we are in "safe mode," our power limited, our focus on warding off the attacks and staying alive, any thoughts of what we really want to do in the world become quite secondary. Make sense? This doesn't mean you don't know what you are here to do. It may, in your case, simply mean you don't feel relaxed, secure and safe enough to really bring it to the light. And that's okay. Release the emotional blocks creating your insecurity and sense of danger, including all the memories, and you will be well on your way to knowing what you really want to do.

Chapter Nineteen...

The second reason we don't know what we want is that we have been programmed to believe that we can't have what we want. One of my Mom's favorite expressions was: "You can't have your cake and eat it too." Really? Why not? Being born of parents who were either born or raised during wartime, what they wanted was quite inconsequential compared to far more serious issues, like whether there was enough food on the table, a safe roof over their head, staying alive, keeping employment, and not getting sick. These were major priorities for many of our parents and grandparents. Consequently, what you wanted to be, do, or have was pretty inconsequential. Nobody paid much attention to those desires, so they weren't fostered or nurtured or developed. For many people, the desires withered and faded away, and the belief became very ingrained in us that it would be a month of Sundays before you got what you wanted. In order words, stop dreaming—it wasn't going to happen.

Perhaps you were a child or youngster who was determined and you did persevere without the support. Most often, you were knocked out somehow and learned that no matter how hard you tried, you didn't get what you wanted. At a Tribal Mentality level, we actually believe that people who get what they want are "lucky," "spoiled," "have the Midas touch," or had some other magical, mystical thing happen to them that could never happen to us. What rubbish! You can have what you want because you are already getting what you want at some level. Your life is a perfect blueprint of what you believe is possible for your life, so you are powerfully creating and manifesting your life already. It's actually quite ridiculous to limit ourselves so we can't have what we want. What you have settled for at some level is what the Tribe thinks you want, your parents think you want, what your religious upbringing thinks you want, or even what your soul thinks it wants to get out of this lifetime. Release that belief that you can't have what you want at a DNA and cellular level, and life can change dramatically. You do deserve to have what you want. You really do.

Ask Yourself:

Is there an incident in your early childhood that stands out as traumatic, painful or disturbing?

To Do:

List the emotions that come up around the incident and let them go at a DNA and cellular level.

Need help?

Go to www.anamazinglifenow.com and claim your free gift just for my readers. The password is the first word of Chapter 31. You'll love the gift.

Chapter Twenty...

Another reason you don't know what you want and may feel stressed, irritable and on that merry-go-round of "my life doesn't work" is because of what I call Divine Discontent.

What is Divine Discontent? Today it's often diagnosed as depression, menopausal symptoms and a host of other physical maladies. However, Divine Discontent is very much a soul issue. It just oftentimes plays out in the body.

Divine Discontent is when you feel a longing in your heart and a yearning in your soul. There's almost a grieving feeling, a deep sadness that you just can't put your finger on. It never leaves you. You wake up in the middle of the night with this sadness. It hits you as you wash your hair in the shower. Sometimes, you feel pissed off and can't explain it—but it doesn't go away. That is what I call Divine Discontent. Perhaps you know it intimately.

It's what happens to us when we haven't found our reason for being. Clarrissa Pinkola Estes in *Women Who Run with the Wolves* calls it *"hambre del alma"*—hunger of the soul. It's strong, it's powerful, it is our soul's drive to identify our Assignment. Remember, your five CEOs. Your soul is here to accomplish something. It has returned for a very specific reason, and oftentimes by the time you are 30 or 40 or 50, it has itchy feet to get things done. It wants to start moving, but by that time you're settled in to a family, a career, a way of being that doesn't always suit your soul's reasons for being here as well as it would like. So the discontent starts—the dissatisfaction, the bitchiness, and the sadness. You go to the doctor, who defines it as depression or menopause or whatever is the malady of the day; and now on some anti-depressant or hormonal treatment, you continue to struggle through. Of course you would. This is not a physical issue. It is a soul issue and needs to be dealt with at a soul level.

So back to the question: What do you really want to do? You'd think it would be easy, wouldn't you? I mean, why can't you just get an Assignment at birth, written in clear, explicit instructions, discussed with your parents so they would foster these desires, gifts and talents in you as you grow up, and everything would be easy as pie. But remember Rudy in the beginning of the book. Rudy knew what his soul wanted to do and he was ignoring it. That Assignment may not be easy. It may stretch your comfort zone, put you out in left field when you want to be safe and secure at home plate. It may test your faith and every bit of trust you have in yourself and a Higher Power. Isn't it perfect? If we aren't here to be stretched, molded, per-fected and used to a greater purpose than we could possibly imagine, then why are we taking up space?

You have chosen to be here at a most crucial time in history, at a time when our very existence is threatened, and your soul decided that it could contribute to our survival, play a critical role, and be part of the solution. What are you waiting for? As has been asked many times, "If not now, when? If not you, who?" The answer is obvious. You are here for a reason, a very special reason, and your Assignment is waiting for you. It's not going anywhere and neither are you. So let's see how perfectly equipped you are to deal with your Assignment, whatever it is, and that may help make it a whole lot easier.

Chapter Twenty-one...

You were born with Sacred Gifts. I am not talking about talents, skills, passions or your Assignment. You were brought into this world with your own unique combination of Sacred Gifts. The concept of Sacred Gifts has been discussed since the age of ancient Egypt.

The Bible talks about them as well, and today many people are learning about their specific Sacred Gifts. I first learned about them from an expert on Sacred Gifts, Monique MacDonald. Monique learned about them from the Catherine of Sienna Institute, which teaches about Sacred Gifts within the Catholic Church. Monique has been teaching people about Sacred Gifts now for more than seven years, and the result never ceases to astound me.

So what is a Sacred Gift?

It is critical to understand that these gifts are in us, but they aren't of us. Why do I say that? Because they are gifts that are given to us at birth by God, as tools that we have access to throughout our lives. They're sacred because of where they come from and they deserve a great deal of reverence and respect. Their primary purpose is to be used to do good in this world.

Our Sacred Gifts empower us with abilities that just can't be explained by what would be considered normal human abilities. They show up, sometimes totally unexpectedly, and allow us to experience results that we just can't even explain.

I am sure that everyone has heard of J.K. Rowling, author of the Harry Potter series. The first person to ever become a billionaire writing books, she was literally a destitute single mother, stuck on a delayed train, when she got the idea of the Harry Potter series. Producing record-breaking best-seller after record-breaking best-seller, it is quite clearly evident that J. K. Rowling has the Sacred Gift of writing.

You may also be familiar with Paul Potts, the British man who took the world by storm, singing opera on a talent show. It was obvious from the crowd's reaction that something supernatural was happening when Paul Potts opened his mouth to sing. What a fabulous demonstration of the Sacred Gift of Music!

But you don't need to become a billionaire author or the next Paul Potts to use your gifts. Doing something as simple and natural to you as having friends in for dinner, preparing an Excel spreadsheet, or being able to sew a beautiful dress without a pattern are all examples of Sacred Gifts.

For example, when the Sacred Gift of Healing showed up most unexpectedly in my life, I was shocked and also uncomfortable. Coming from a background as one of Jehovah's Witnesses, it felt a bit "wooey-wooey" to be able to see inside a person's physical body, read their thoughts, and see their past lives as clearly as watching a movie picture. Yet the good that was happening for others was evident. Because I knew about Sacred Gifts at the time, I was able to accept and embrace my Sacred Gift.

There are several Sacred Gifts—24 to be exact, according to Monique. You may have the Sacred Gift of teaching, of being a visionary, of hospitality, or of feeling compelled to pray for others, or you may have the Sacred Gift of singleness such as Oprah Winfrey enjoys. These Sacred Gifts come to you so naturally that you may be inclined to believe they are "normal," "typical" and "usual." I mean, can't everybody write a book in a month? Doesn't everybody want to help the homeless? Can't everybody plan an event for 1000 people and love every minute of it? No, not necessarily. You have Sacred Gifts within you to support your Assignment. When you learn about your Sacred Gifts, you will be astounded at how life begins to make sense. You stop beating yourself up for what you don't do well, stop judging yourself severely for what you do do well, and stop criticizing others for what they don't like to do. You will be a much nicer person and much easier to live with both for yourself and for everyone around you.

Have you ever noticed that some people are naturally charismatic? People love to be around them, they are like magnets, successful and charming. They may seem happier than you, and they feel light energetically. They're not stressed out and hating life. They seem to have found an Aladdin's lamp. What's their secret? The origin of the English word "charismatic" can shed some light on this. It derives from the Greek word charism, meaning **"a Divine gift believed to be given by God or a Spiritual Endowment**." When someone is operating from their gifts or their charisms, they are powerfully charismatic and effective. Do you want to be charismatic, magnetic and charming? Start operating from your Sacred Gifts and it's amazing how your energy can shift to the positive!

So what are some of the characteristics of a Sacred Gift? The first and foremost important characteristic of Sacred Gifts is that they are given to us to be of benefit to others. They are always, always, always for the benefit of others, **without** exception. This is one of the distinguishing aspects between a Sacred Gift and a skill or a talent. While a talent might be to your benefit, a Gift is for the benefit of others.

Because these gifts may only show up when others need them from you, this might explain why you can be really good at doing something for others, but that very same area in your own personal life can be screwed up. You might be incredibly organized at work and your house is a disorganized mess. You might be very gifted at creating budgets and systems, yet your own checkbook isn't even balanced. A mechanic might love and be totally energized by fixing other people's cars, yet his own car barely runs because he just can't get motivated to fix it.

Understanding your Sacred Gifts allows you to operate from a place of confidence, joy and contentment. Now that I know my Sacred Gifts, I can let go of the rest of my life without the guilt. How many times do you beat yourself up because you think you should be better at something than you are? You think you should enjoy doing something more than you do. I used to try to do stupid things like my own accounting simply because I had taken an accounting course. I used to try to do my own flyers simply because I had bought a software program that was "For Dummies"! That one really hurt when I couldn't produce a single decent flyer!

Today I do ONLY what I love and I give others the joy of doing what they love. Trust me, there are people who love to do the bookkeeping, there are people who love Excel spreadsheets, and there are people who love formatting flyers. I find people who have the same passion for those jobs as I do for writing, for teaching, and for healing. As a matter of fact, when I am looking for help, I actually say, "For the right person this job will be fun and easy…" In other words, I am looking for someone who has the Sacred Gift to accomplish the job I want done.

It's fascinating and saddening to watch people do things they don't like and aren't good at, to see how it stresses them because they have a belief they should be good at everything. They think, "If I can fix a car, I can make a soufflé." "If I am an excellent assistant to the Chairman of the Board, I would make a great CEO." What an absolute untruth!

The Peter Principle states that in a hierarchy we eventually reach the limit of our abilities, and once that limit is exceeded, we begin to fail and operate from a place of incompetence. But it's more than that. Someone may have the Sacred Gift of Service and love to help out the workshop facilitator, do for them, run for them, be completely in service and be totally brilliant. But put them in the role of the facilitator and unless they have the Sacred Gift of Facilitation, they may bomb. It has nothing to do with competence and reaching the top of our ladder. It has everything to do with what our Sacred Gifts are, full stop, period.

Once you understand your Sacred Gifts, you have the ability to understand completely why you love what you do, why it comes so naturally to you, and why you just don't want to do other things. You can now be guilt-free when you say, "I'd love to help you organize the party, but my real gift lays in decorating the room. Can I do that for you instead?" Or "A better use of my gift would be to write out the welcome speech for you rather than be the greeter at the door."

If you have ever been to an event and the person handing out the programs doesn't have the Sacred Gift of Service or the Sacred Gift of Hospitality, you'll notice it. And if the person does have one or both of those gifts, you'll surely notice that! Think of the people who really stand out in your mind as being energetic and joyful, on top of a project, exceptionally good at anything from hosting a dinner party to hairdressing to speaking to a riveted audience. That's where you want to be in your life. Focus on utilizing your Sacred Gifts in your life to the benefit of others and you will be amazed at how energized you feel, how happy you are and how you can say, no, no, no, no, no, no and no to what are NOT your Sacred Gifts easily and effortlessly without the fear, doubt and guilt.

Curious? Fascinated?

If you want to know about YOUR Sacred Gifts, go to www.yoursacredgifts.com and find out more.

Chapter Twenty-two...

Many people would love to get off the merry-go-round of stress, of doing what they hate, and of feeling overwhelmed because of not feeling "good enough"—but a big fear stops them: the feeling that it's selfish to just do what you want. Won't people think you're egotistical if you just do what you're good at and delegate the rest? Aren't you being self-centered to want life to be that easy?

Please stop. I'm laughing too hard. The idea that living an amazing life of little to no stress, happiness and joy is selfish, self-centered and egotistical is such a product of what I call Tribal Mentality—it's pathetic and ridiculous.

The Tribe isn't particularly happy—or haven't you noticed? If you're too happy, they get edgy around you. They think you're strange, or that you must be on the latest anti-depressant mixed with some other prescription cocktail. Being naturally happy these days is certainly not natural by the Tribe's standards. *Easy, stress-free* and *joyful* are words we fling around like *green revolution, find your passion* and *social entrepreneur.* But few people really seem to get what they mean. They sound good, but nobody actually expects you to change the environment, do what you love and revolutionize the world while you're at it. "Nice thought," they might say, "but get real!"

So if you walk around happy, doing what you love, smiling at life and saying no without any guilt, know that people will think you're strange. They may admire you, find you curious, even envy you, but they probably won't understand you. I mean isn't the stress of fighting rush-hour every day for hours to go sit in unhealthy offices natural? Isn't eating at fast food chains regularly, being in massive debt and morbidly overweight perfectly normal? NO, it's not! But it is a brave soul that gets out of the Tribe, finds their happiness, and says goodbye to the scarcity thinking and struggling mentality of the Tribe.

Jane phoned me, quite upset. Her friends all thought her life was too simple and she needed to take her finances more seriously, save to buy a house and work harder. She was feeling guilty because she really was happy with her life. A perfect day to her was teaching an exercise class, spending time with her son, having lunch with friends, making a nice dinner and then spending time volunteering at her community church. I asked her to do a simple exercise.

"Make a list of what you really want to do," I said. "Then go through the list and really check in with yourself as to whether or not you are writing that thing down because you *believe* you should want it, you'd feel *guilty* if it wasn't on your list because it ought to be, or it's truly someone else's dream, goal or vision. Scratch anything that falls into one of those categories. Then look at what is left. Double-check that everything on that list is *your* passion, what lights *your* fire and what gets *you* excited. Anything less than that— scratch it!"

At the end of the exercise, Jane found herself with only a few things on her list. The next time we spoke, she noted to me how challenging it had been to just focus on what she wanted and ignore all the little voices in her head that told her she should want and desire more things. She really wanted a simple life. Family, friends, church, teaching exercise classes, working with individual clients and facilitating workshops. I cleared the emotions of fear, doubt and guilt so she could be content with her desire for a simple life.

What happened since she got her own desires really clear? Her exercise classes were better than ever, and she was already beginning to be asked to do more of them. She had acquired three new clients in less than two weeks. AND a major corporation had approached her about facilitating workshops for their international company. PLUS she had deposited more money in her bank account in one single day than she had in months! She was ecstatic.

Simplicity is a Sacred Gift. Those who have it do not want a mansion, a Martha Stewart empire, or a Porsche in the driveway. Leading an amazing life doesn't mean the same thing to everyone, and that is a good thing. The only thing that's important is that you get very clear on what an amazing life looks like to you!

So please, please, please understand that the belief that leading an incredible life makes you self-centered and egotistical is absolutely false. Let go of that belief right now and KNOW in every cell of your body that you deserve to have a wonderful life, an incredible life, a peaceful life, a joyful life, a tranquil life, and abundance, overflow and prosperity.

It's not just your right to live life as fully as possible. It's your responsibility. Why do I say that?

To Do:

- ✓ Make a list of what you really want to do in your life.
- ✓ Review the list as you check in as to whether or not YOU really want what you wrote down.
- ✓ Eliminate everything you wrote down that is there to please someone else.
- ✓ Cross off anything you included because of fear or guilt.
- ✓ Remove something if you don't get excited just thinking about doing it.
- ✓ Now talk to somebody else about it and notice your level of passion.
- ✓ Anything less than a 10 on the passion scale, throw out!

Chapter Twenty-three...

In *A Return to Love*, Marianne Williamson wrote: "As you let your own light shine, you unconsciously give other people permission to do the same. As you are liberated from your own fear, your presence automatically liberates others."

The greatest gift you can give to others is to get off the merry-go-round of playing small, pretending to be much less powerful than you truly are, and not living life fully. The more you shine, the more you will feel satisfied, happy, fulfilled and joyful, and the less you will feel threatened or resentful when someone has a success that is not yours. People are often nasty, miserable, snarky and rude with others because they feel threatened by their success. There is a saying that there are two ways to have the tallest building in the city. One is to build one taller than any other; the other way is to tear everything else down. People do the latter all the time. They tear other people down so they can look and feel important. We see this often in corporations, families and politics. It's ridiculous because it is a merry-go-round of "I'm not good enough" nonsense, the "I am not deserving" crap, and the "I must be perfect" rubbish.

The problem with that merry-go-round is there is NO end to it. For example, just 46 days after Roger Bannister finally broke the four-minute mile in 1954, someone broke his brand-new record. Do you get this? No matter how wonderful you are, how much you do for others, how much you give, it will never, ever, ever be enough as long as you believe that you aren't good enough. Volunteer for one charity and people will ask why you can't volunteer for two. Create an income of $250,000 a year and you'll wonder why you can't make $500,000. After years of trying to beat the four-minute mile and finally doing so, Bannister surely didn't expect his new record to be broken in less than two months. Imagine the pressure then to…what, run a three-and-a-half-minute mile? a three-minute mile? Really, what comes next?

It's a classic merry-go-round, and it can only create stress, fear, and a lot of unhappiness in your life. Accept that you are amazing, and that everyone else is as well, and life shifts dramatically. Once you get comfortable with how wonderful you are, then the nit-picking, witchy-bitchiness of criticism, judgment and hatred can finally end. LOVE YOURSELF is your new mantra for life—which leads me to another critical point.

To Do:

Read this out loud and notice the shift when it is said in the first person:

"As I let my own light shine, I unconsciously give other people permission to do the same. As I am liberated from my own fear, my presence automatically liberates others."

Chapter Twenty-four...

You are the most important person in your life.

I can just hear you now: "Now THAT is taking this to the limit," "No way," "Impossible," "Can't buy into this one," "Now you've gone too far." Go ahead—vent all of your anger around this one. Get it out of your system, because it needs to get out. I will say it again: You are the most important person in your life. Without this as a foundation of your belief system, your life will never work.

Let me explain. Have you ever flown on an airplane? What does the flight attendant say when they are going through the safety procedures: "Put your oxygen mask on first before you assist anyone else." True, or true? Well the same applies in your life. You need to put your own oxygen mask on first. Why does the flight attendant say this? Because if you go to help a child or an elderly person without first securing your oxygen mask, you will end up out of breath and of no use to anyone. Put your oxygen mask on FIRST and you will be able to help, with no restrictions or limitations.

It's really very simple. We understand that on the plane. Can we understand that in your life? You need to put your oxygen mask on first in life. To do that, you need to understand, at a DNA and cellular level, that you are the MOST important person in your life. Until you look after yourself, you will be extremely limited in how you can look after others. I've seen many entrepreneurs who spend all their time organizing fundraisers and helping others grow their businesses without knowing how they will get the money to pay their own phone bill. Yes, you may have the Sacred Gift of Service, but that doesn't change a thing. You have to look after yourself first and foremost.

When I didn't have a pot to pee in financially, I was off raising money for charities. I had $100 to my name, no credit rating, no one to turn to for help, and I was living in a cabin with no heat and rats running up and down the walls. Only then did I realize that this was NOT the life I envisioned for myself. It certainly didn't feel good on several levels. It was at that moment I realized that a very strong belief that "my needs weren't important" had to change.

It's not that I hadn't heard the right advice. One of my millionaire girlfriends had repeatedly said to me, "Put your own oxygen mask on first, Jan." But it wasn't until I hit rock bottom for the second time that I paid attention to her words and actually did something about it. So yes, I understand you may want to save the whales, feed the children, and help the environment. I get that. But by looking after yourself first, you will do so with complete peace, relaxation, freedom and joy rather than stress, guilt, doubt and fear.

So what does looking after yourself really entail? Let's talk about that—because we're usually not very good at it.

Chapter Twenty-five...

Remember your body CEO? Well, it has a lot to say. Perhaps you've noticed. It lets you know when it is tired, hungry, thirsty, or in need of other vital bodily functions. But other than feeling ravenous, tired or knowing you need to go to the bathroom, what else is your body telling you? Lots!

Your body, in cooperation with your Subconscious Mind, is constantly looking after you. Thank God most of us don't need to think about every heartbeat or breath of air. It all happens automatically. Cells are replaced constantly, so every seven years we have a completely new body. Those cells are workhorses for us. They do everything from digestion, assimilation and elimination, to the processing of thoughts and emotions.

Imagine you had a donkey. You put one pack on that donkey and off it goes. But what would happen if you loaded on 10, 20 or 30 packs? Would the donkey have the same energy and ability to move? Obviously not! So now imagine your cells as that donkey. You put a bit of worry into your life—that's one pack. Then you go out and party for the night and you eat and drink lots of things that are stressful to the body. Two more packs. That night you only get a few hours of sleep—another pack. Then in the morning, you don't eat because you feel sick. Another pack. Instead, you sit at the computer all day and talk on your cell phone. Two more packs. Maybe a cigarette or a soft drink—more packs. Then there's the fear about the upcoming doctor's appointment—another pack. Are you getting the picture? Our poor little cells end up with the packs of our living habits and all of our emotions, and eventually, like that overloaded donkey, they can't do their job any longer. They are so bombarded with emotions, chemicals, toxins and toxic thoughts that they go into what my partner, a medical doctor, calls "immune confusion." They don't know which

          Getting Off the Merry-Go-Round

way is up, who's the enemy, or what to do next. Finally we end up with an autoimmune disease such as AIDS, rheumatoid arthritis, fibromyalgia, or a host of other diseases such as cancer, heart disease or depression.

The cells in our body, so perfectly designed to work for us, protect us and repair us, can't even budge for all the garbage they have to deal with. That energetic donkey, loaded down with 100 backpacks, lays down and dies. And so do we.

I'm no medical doctor, but I can tell you what I "see" inside the bodies of my clients. The cells are spinning erratically, furiously trying to rid themselves of these burdens, frantically trying to do their work. As I work with a client and we unload these packs of emotions, thoughts, beliefs, and programs, the cells eagerly dump these toxic packages and feel lighter—and much, much happier.

Can it really happen that simply?

All I have ever cared about is results. When you are broke, homeless, and a mess emotionally, there is only one thing that counts, and that is results. So what I will tell you is that the results are there for me and for my clients. They feel lighter at a cellular level.

As I was putting my life back together and spending thousands of hours in the lab with God to understand why it seemed so challenging, my argument with God amounted to this: the changes needed to be easy. If it was very easy for me to do Program A in my life—which included being a poor, controlling, impatient, perfectionist bitch and slob, and all of those things happened automatically, then could it not be as easy to run Program B in my life? The answer was yes, but then I needed to release and reprogram at a cellular level.

So Program B was slowly installed as Program A was eliminated. Program B included being nice automatically, being abundant automatically, being non-judgmental and patient automatically, being in the flow automatically and being tidy automatically. It certainly did not all happen overnight, but the results showed up bit by bit—automatically. Anything less than automatic is way too much work in my opinion. With as many things as I needed to work on in my life to get it to where I wanted it to be, I could have spent all day doing affirmations, snapping my wrist with a rubber band for every negative thought until it was red and bleeding, or at counselors, workshops or reading self-help books all day. I simply wasn't willing to tap, snap or affirm for the rest of my life. I needed help fast AND easy. So one of the easiest ways to look after yourself is to release these negative beliefs, programs and emotions at a cellular level.

But there's more.

To Do:

Look at your day and see what "backpacks" you are putting on your cells? Here are some examples to get you started:

- Late night
- No breakfast
- Fast food lunch
- Dinner out of the microwave
- Not enough water
- At the computer all day
- Sat in rush hour traffic for 2 hours

Decide in what area(s) you can begin to unload the burden on your body.

Chapter Twenty-Six…

The other day as I was walking along the beach for my routine twilight walk, I watched a beautiful golden retriever fetch a ball and then run straight into the ocean and lay down. The wave came in around him and his whole tummy was now bathed in cool water. He lay there for a few waves and just enjoyed the rest. His owner shrugged his shoulders as if to say, "Not much I can do." I laughed out loud as this long-haired dog had the sense to do something about the heat. He got himself to a place where it was cool.

It's a shame more of us don't have the same sense. I often work with clients who are burned out, frazzled, and exhausted, and then they'll get on the phone with me and tell me that this year they want to earn a million dollars, find a new love and lose 40 pounds. It's hard not to laugh out loud. Are you really serious? For you to create a life that is full of joy, love, peace and prosperity, you need some fuel in the tank, folks. Without any fuel in the tank, you are not getting out of the garage!

Your body is your vehicle for this lifetime. It is a Rolls-Royce if you let it be, but many people treat it like it is a broken-down old farm tractor. If you are pushing yourself beyond the limit, working too many hours, not taking time off for play, eating all the wrong foods, keeping yourself going with coffee, stimulants or alcohol, getting by with little sleep on top of massive amounts of stress, and then wondering why you don't feel good—give your head a shake! You take better care of your car than you do of yourself!

So the body eventually says, "ENOUGH!" and you collapse. You end up breaking something, so you are forced to take time off, you end up with a disease that helps you set very new priorities, or you end up with energy so low that brushing your teeth every morning feels like an accomplishment. BEFORE you get to that level, why not take care of yourself? Imagine having a racehorse that is going to run in the Kentucky Derby. But the racehorse is overweight, out of shape and hasn't been out of the stall for six months. That horse may drag its rear end around the track with a whole lot of prodding, but it ain't going to win any races, much less the Big One. Are you that racehorse? It's great to want to accomplish a lot in your life but the vehicle, your body, absolutely has to be in the race with you. Without it, you will drag your butt through life, complaining, moaning and groaning and feeling like you are carrying an anchor weighing about 1000 pounds.

People think that simple things like eating fruits, vegetables and protein, sleeping eight hours a day, drinking pure water and exercising a minimum of three times per week are luxuries. In fact, these things are necessities. You don't think that putting fuel in your car is a luxury, do you? You don't think that changing the oil regularly is a luxury. These are necessities for your car. So what about you? Are you less important? If you are treating yourself as if you are, then you are getting results to match.

You may not like those results, but they follow directly from getting on that merry-go-round of "no time to eat properly," "no time to exercise," "no time to sleep eight hours"—beliefs that we need to let go. Your body is amazing and it will provide you the means to do what you need to do in this life, but you absolutely cannot take it for granted. We are in a health crisis and for good reason. Bodies are exhausted and losing the race. Death at 40, 50 and even younger is no longer unusual. I know of six people under 60 who have died from natural causes in the last six months. They weren't hit by a car or run over by a train. They died from cancer, heart disease, or failure of the immune system to protect them from infection. I don't want to scare you, but think about it—if you are abusing your body by considering proper diet, adequate sleep, sufficient water and some exercise to be luxuries, you are headed down the same path. Our bodies are under far too much pressure today from emotions, toxins and stress to not be operating at full power. Let go of the belief that you don't have time to look after yourself, because you may be more right than you want to be.

Our body also appreciates when we ask for permission or forgiveness and show appreciation. Once again, the experience of my clients can demonstrate this.

Joyce had had back surgery and a plate installed in her back. However, after her back healed, she complained to me of stomach problems. In a healing session, I realized that her stomach was angry at not being asked for permission to be moved during surgery and had never been thanked for the healing it had contributed to. We took care of those issues and the stomach pain went away.

Michael had a shunt inserted into his body to help his kidney function properly. The shunt was causing Michael a lot of pain. I asked the body to accept the shunt as part of its team, asked for forgiveness that it hadn't been asked to accept it much earlier, and thanked the kidney for accepting the invasion. Already while on the call with me, the pain subsided for Michael.

Truth or fantasy? I don't know—I can only talk about the clear results of working with the body. I have helped clients heal scars, regulate bowel movements and even stop biting their nails. I see that every cell in our body has its own separate identity. Each has its role, and by communicating with it as the intelligent organism that it is, it responds beautifully. Scientists are just beginning to understand the intelligence of the DNA and the versatility of the cells, but from my experience, we are only scratching the surface of what cells are capable of accomplishing for us. Start appreciating and caring for your body and you will be amazed at what it can do for you.

To Do:

Note what your beliefs are around health.

To get you started here are some ideas:

- I don't have time to exercise.
- Vegetables taste awful.
- I can't eat first thing in the morning.
- I need coffee to keep going.
- Walking is boring.

Start to release and let go of these disempowering beliefs at a DNA and cellular level.

Stuck on exactly how to do that?

Visit www.anamazinglifenow.com and claim your free gift which will help you get started. The password is the first word of Chapter 31.

Chapter Twenty-Seven...

Sometimes people who have been on the personal development journey will hear about their "inner children." In working with various healers, I was introduced to little Jannie, my own inner child who was upset about this and that. She was usually about eight years old. I was told I needed to talk to Jannie, to placate her and let her know she was loved and safe. I would remember to talk to Jannie for one day—if she was lucky—and then I'd forget. I barely had time to call my best friend and talk to her and here I was supposed to be talking to some inner child who was upset with what happened when I was eight years old! Then she'd pop out again and I would find myself dealing with that precocious, fearful, and vocal child at some of the most inopportune times. She could be most embarrassing as she whined, threw temper tantrums and felt completely vulnerable.

Do we actually believe there is a little girl inside of us, who is three, four, or eight years old? Not literally—but when we refer to "inner children" it sounds as if we do. They are "stuck emotions." Nothing more, nothing less. We will sometimes say, "He's acting like a two-year-old." You're absolutely right—he is. But why? Because a situation triggered a memory of when he was two, and he now feels unsafe, scared, attacked, or in pain, reacting exactly the way the two-year-old reacted, like that emotion is frozen in time. I don't placate inner children (stuck emotions). I simply believe we need to heal that memory and the emotion attached to it and fully integrate the preferred emotion into our Subconscious Mind.

When someone says, "I don't like what you've done," rather than pull a file that says, "I'm bad and unworthy" with an emotion of "fear," we can release that memory and change the file to, "So you don't like what I've done. I did my best and even though you don't like my action, I am still an amazing human being. I just didn't act in accord with what you expected. However, those were your expectations and I'm still just fine, thank you." There is a massive difference between those two emotional responses, wouldn't you agree?

By releasing these stuck emotions, you can change your response to situations that in the past caused fear, doubt, worry, shame and guilt. So connect with that little girl or boy inside of you and have a chat about the emotional issue. Identify it and let it go. It will literally produce a life that is far more stable, far more pleasant and far more even-keeled.

Ask Yourself:

What attitudes and emotions do you display that resemble those of a child?

1. How do you respond to criticism?

2. How do you react to a crisis?

3. What is your reaction to authority?

4. How do you respond to fear?

5. What is your response to the opposite sex?

Start releasing them because as cute as a kid can be, it isn't so cute at your age.

Chapter Twenty-Eight...

So have you decided what you want your life to really look like? Do you perhaps have a vision board or a list of the 101 things you really want to do? Has getting this far in the book helped you to appreciate some of the beliefs that have been hindering you from having a more amazing life? What do you want?

You don't need to move to another country to be happy, you know. I was a very happy person in Vancouver, Canada. I just love where I live right now. You may simply need to do a few things differently. Perhaps you are feeling pretty sick right now on the merry-go-round of large mortgage payments for a house you can't afford. What about downsizing? Do you really need all that space, or are you keeping it out of obligation, fear, or worry about what other people will think? Could you live in a different part of the country where the cost of living is cheaper? That was my question: Why am I living in one of the most expensive cities in the world when I can do my work anywhere? There are less expensive places to live in your own city or country. Might one of those be an option for you?

Remember to start thinking about how to create the life you want, rather than why you can't do it. Do you want to leave a religion that is no longer providing you the support it once did or whose beliefs no longer match your own? What's keeping you there? When Stephen and I decided to leave the Jehovah's Witnesses, it was a tough decision that took three full years to make. We realized the repercussions were tremendous and weighed our decision carefully. But at the end of the day, we just knew that we could no longer stay. The shoe no longer fit, and it was giving us major blisters! We were well aware that there would be a price to pay. Friends would never talk to us again, our parents would be devastated, and our marriage would no longer have the foundation of a very strict rule on divorce. It would be a bit scary negotiating life without the familiar parameters that we had been raised with. Everything, and I mean everything, would now be open for discussion and decision. It was definitely a big task.

However, we also looked at the benefits. I had been forbidden for ten years to speak with my favorite sister who had been kicked out of the religion. I could now associate with her freely. We realized that our available time would now be immense as the over-scheduled life of a Jehovah's Witness fell away. We focused on the positive and decided it clearly outweighed the negative. I have never regretted the decision despite the hell that broke loose afterward in my life. Heaven did follow that hell—and it's a magnificent place.

Leaving a marriage or relationship may be another tough decision you need to make. Many people stay in loveless, abusive and dead marriages and relationships because they are afraid to move on and out. It's comfortable and safe, even if that means no sex, emotional abuse or financial hardship. Remember that your team of five CEOs is primarily concerned about safety—everything else is a bonus. But you can be safe and still not happy, successful or abundant, so the program around safety has to be expanded to include more than the basics.

Pat is staying in her marriage because she doesn't want to leave her house and animals. They mean more to her than her own happiness. John is staying in his marriage because he doesn't have time to deal with the upheaval of separation and divorce, especially as he has a young daughter. Laura is staying in her unsatisfactory relationship because, at her age, she doesn't know if she'll find anything better. Are you staying in a marriage or relationship you would like to get out of but don't know how? Look at the beliefs, programs and emotions you have attached to this situation. You're probably afraid. You are most likely overwhelmed at the repercussions. You very well could feel powerless to change the situation because you are financially entangled. Guilt is also a powerful force, as your decision has ramifications throughout the immediate family, extended family and even the community. You may feel depressed because you believe divorce is a statement to the world that you are a failure. You may feel trapped because divorce isn't allowed in your religion.

Take the time to examine your reasons for staying in a situation that isn't working. Susan cried on the phone to me that she was going to hell because she had an affair and now wanted a divorce. She had tried to work things out with her husband but now felt repulsed by him, angry and frustrated. Susan is not going to make her life or the life of her children peaceful, joyful, loving or prosperous by staying. All of her attention and energy is focused on dealing with a very draining and negative situation. She needs to get off the merry-go-round of fear, doubt and guilt and move on. In connecting energetically with her children, every one of them communicated to me their frustration, anger and their fervent desire for their parents to divorce and move on. They would only benefit from a firm resolve on Susan's part to move ahead in her life so they could be freed of the negative energy that fighting, yelling and arguing brought to the family.

If you believe you can't leave a difficult marriage or relationship because of fear, doubt or guilt, please know right now it is a lie you are telling yourself because you are afraid to do what you need to do. You doubt your ability to handle and cope with the new situation and are therefore choosing to feel guilty about putting your own happiness first in your life. Only you can change that, and I highly recommend you do sooner rather than later.

I told Susan that when we vowed at our marriage ceremony to be committed to this person till "death do us part," it didn't necessarily mean our physical death. Perhaps what it meant was the death of our love for that person. We really need to let go of the belief that we need to endure a loveless marriage for the children, or we need to stay in an abusive relationship because of our vow to God, or that we are self-centered and wicked to want love, joy and peace in our life. Great soap opera material, but not great for real-life living. Leave the drama to afternoon television and move into a life that feels good and right for you.

Chapter Twenty-Nine...

Moving into a life that feels right for you might actually mean more than just changing beliefs, letting go of some old programs, and releasing at a cellular level. You might actually need to pick up and physically move your home to achieve your desired lifestyle. Sometimes a move to another house, community or city will be all that it takes to give you that fresh start, but what if your soul, like Rudy's soul, longs for more than just a move across town. What if you do want to live in a tropical place, swing on hammocks and walk the beach at sunset every night? Is it really possible to get off the merry-go-round of life in a highly developed country and make a life in a less-developed country? It certainly is. One of the biggest questions you need to answer is: Do you still need to produce an annual income to do that? In my case, I do. So then how are you going to produce that annual income?

You may be able to work full-time for six months and then spend six months in another, less expensive country. That would probably mean adjusting your cost of living and saving enough to live six months with no income. Or you can do what I have done. With technology as it is, I simply transferred my business to Mexico. I do all of my work on the phone via the computer or writing on the computer, so I needed just one component to work for me—high speed Internet.

In the condo I am currently living in, I had high speed Internet installed and use technology such as Skype and a VOIP (Voice Over Internet Protocol) phone system that is completely linked to my computer. The condo also has a landline with a Mexican phone number, so if for some reason the Internet doesn't work, I can give my clients a Personal Identification Number (PIN) for a long-distance calling card (all bought online) and they can call me. The cost is about 2.5 cents a minute. My clients know that I am living in Mexico, but I have a U.S. phone number on my VOIP phone so my friends don't have to call Mexico.

Your priority in living abroad is to determine what you want in your new life. If you want to live with all of the amenities of "home," if you want all of your friends around you on a regular basis, and you want life to be "just like home," then stay home. You will be unhappy in another country for any length of time. Having said that, you can currently find in many developing countries much of what we accept as normal in a developed country. I am currently living in Mazatlán. There is a Sam's Club here, a Wal-Mart Super Centre, Home Depot, Office Depot, movie theatres, fine restaurants, and just about everything one could want for shopping. However, despite all of that, this is still not home, and you need to remember that. People drive like maniacs. You can forget about suing anybody if something goes wrong. Time has a whole different meaning. And if you don't speak Spanish, there will be times you will feel frustrated. But every morning when I get up to the sun shining in that robin egg blue sky, the waves crashing beautifully on the shore, and a gracious Mexican person, a complete stranger, going out of their way to help me, I feel blessed to live here. Every day that I get to write, coach, heal and remember I am a guest in a most magnificent country, I thank God.

That doesn't mean it's perfect. It doesn't have to be. I miss my friends, my partner and a certain standard of living. The water here is never quite hot enough, I can't bop out for dinner with my best friend, and my partner can't easily come spend the weekend with me. It can be lonely; there can be culture shock. But an open mind goes a long way.

Ask yourself what you really want in your new life. Do you want the best weather? Is being close to excellent medical facilities important? Is speaking the language crucial for you? Is the cost of living the most critical? Do some travelling to various places and see what feels right for you. You may think you'd be fine in a country where you don't speak the language, but when you feel like a two-year-old who can't communicate with someone, that may not be so charming. You may want sunshine and heat, but when it's 105 degrees Fahrenheit in the shade and your earlobes are sweating (along with other parts of your body that you didn't know could sweat), will you be envious of the rain, gray skies and snow back home? You may think that being alone without a soul to bother you would be heaven on earth, but try spending a week alone with no one to talk to and see how it feels. You may not enjoy your own company nearly as much as you thought. Perhaps you have dreamed of just doing "nothing," but that novelty can wear off pretty darn quick after a few days of it. "Nothing" can be boring once you've read a few books, napped for a week, and stared at the ocean for several afternoons. But let's say you really do want to hit warmer climes, spend time with yourself, and learn to relax at a whole new level. What next?

Questions to Ask:

- Do you need to produce an income?

- Can your current business be transferred to another country with some adjustments and use of technology?

- What's really important to you in your new life?

Chapter Thirty...

I know I will not spend the rest of my life in Mazatlán. As a matter of fact, my partner and I just rented a gorgeous condo outside of Puerto Vallarta for next winter, but right now Mazatlán suits me for many purposes. It is very convenient to return to the Seattle area where my partner currently lives. One day of flying, one stop in LA and about $500 and I'm back in familiar territory with Greg. A three-hour coach ride and I'm back in Canada with old friends and can speak or attend a workshop. That's important to me right now as I will return approximately four times this year for speaking engagements and to assist at business workshops. Being on roughly the same time zone is also critical as I don't want to travel sixteen hours and be jet-lagged for several days. Think about this as you plan your getaway.

The technology in Mazatlán is also sufficiently advanced for me to look after clients while here. My Mexican Internet service costs an affordable $26 per month. I feel safe and secure, which is important as I am living alone. I pay $1000 per month for a one-bedroom condo on the beach, including electricity, water, gas, phone and weekly maid service. On Saturdays, Señora Tomy comes in to clean my place, change my linens, and take out my garbage, leaving the place sparkling clean. So what does it cost for me to live here per month?

Living a very nice lifestyle, complete with manicures, pedicures, massages, taxi service when I need it, and covering my business expenses in North America such as storage, website maintenance, shopping cart, hosting, etc., it costs me approximately $2,500. That includes a $400 allowance per month for traveling back to North America four times per year. I could live cheaper but I don't need to scrimp and so I don't. I have heard of couples easily living on that amount, depending where they live in Mexico, but $30,000 per year to live my lifestyle is well within my budget.

So what emotions are coming up for you as you read this? Are you excited, scared, nervous, doubtful—or anxious to just get started?

To Do:

Start investigating your options. International Living (www.internationalliving.com) is a great place to start if living abroad is your desire.

Ask Yourself:

What emotions come up for me as I contemplate moving to another city, country or making a major adjustment in life?

Getting Off the Merry-Go-Round

Chapter Thirty-One...

Brenda and Adrian love to travel. They have travelled the world and every year are jaunting here and there and everywhere. It's hard to keep up with them. What country are they in now? Would you like to know how do they do it? Brenda is a very successful nutritional counselor with decades of experience behind her in the field of helping women deal with hormonal issues. In working with Brenda, we looked at how she could create leveraged income, let go of some control, delegate and create a lifestyle that worked for them. So they have vacations during which the office runs everything and Brenda is definitely "on holiday" and other vacations during which she will spend a small portion of each day answering emails and being in contact with the office. Recently, she spent 10 days in Hawaii. From 7:00 to 10:00 a.m. each day she handled the business while Adrian made breakfast and got everything ready for a day at the beach. Then off for a day of fun and sun while leaving the daily operation of the business to very competent, trained help.

Brenda was ecstatic upon returning home. "I LOVE my life," she said. "I feel so abundant in having created exactly the lifestyle I wanted."

Did this lifestyle come overnight? No, it didn't. Brenda and Adrian have worked diligently at creating this lifestyle. They have a very solid marital relationship as a foundation, Brenda is a brilliant businesswoman, and they knew where to ask for some guidance and direction. But in speaking with Brenda about how they created the lifestyle she loves, she would say that first of all they got very clear about what they wanted. They had taken off a year to travel, selling everything and closing down the business. As much as they had enjoyed the year, it was also a pain having to start all over again. Living with Dad until they got re-established wasn't the easiest—moving home in your 40s is rarely easy, especially with a husband and daughter. So this time, they were clearer on what they wanted.

They bought a home with an office and with storage facilities to house their nutritional products. Brenda had to give up some control and learn to ask for help. It wasn't easy, but it was crucial for the success of their plan. They hired part-time help and then took the plunge for Adrian to quit his job and join Brenda full-time in the business. And their income increased! That was a relief for them to see, but then they were also committed to making this work. Adrian didn't quit work and then go fishing every day. He learned the ropes of the business and became a huge support so Brenda could focus on what she does well.

Next they set up an easy product for leveraged income in their Total Health Pack and started marketing the daily supplement packages. Brenda had to learn some new communication methods as she set herself up with Skype and fully utilized brilliant technology that allows you to run your business from practically anywhere in the world. Testing the system by leaving on holidays was also part of the plan, then restructuring and re-evaluating what worked and what didn't was part of coming home.

          Getting Off the Merry-Go-Round

Today, they aren't fully where they want to be, but what a far cry from five days a week in a practice with two weeks vacation that many professionals settle for!

What was imperative to make several vacations in a year possible for Brenda and Adrian?

- Clarity about what they wanted.

- Willingness to work outside the box and outside their comfort zone to make it happen.

- Ability to let go of control and delegate.

- Patience that this wouldn't happen overnight or even necessarily in six months.

- Appreciating that perfection is not mandatory or even desirable.

- Extraordinary communication between them in all areas of their life.

- Setting financial priorities. They don't spend a lot of money on frivolous expenditures but put money away regularly for travel.

And perhaps the greatest asset going for them is Brenda and Adrian's ability to go and have fun. No point creating the magical life and then sitting on a beach in Hawaii, worried sick about the order that needed to go out today. Is creating the life you want doable, even when all your ducks aren't lined up in a row? Even when you don't have a million dollars in the bank? Or when you have a business to run? Absolutely!

Next on the agenda for Brenda and Adrian? Watch out, Italy!

Chapter Thirty-Two...

Brenda has mentioned to me several times how the influence of others has dramatically impacted their ability to do what they want. We are all influenced by people. Parents, media, religious leaders, friends, business colleagues, and even our neighbors all impact our life. Ask yourself if you are happy with their impact. They may be a big part of the problem, part of the reason your life isn't working, or they might be a big part of why your life can work.

It is really critical that you surround yourself with people who support you on your journey in a positive way. You don't need naysayers in your life who will pooh-pooh every idea you have or tell you you're dreaming way too big. You don't need people who will come up with every reason why you can't have an amazing life. Choose friends who will celebrate your achievements, who aren't envious of your successes and who are not jealous of the changes you are making in your life. Be very clear in your determination that your life is fabulous, incredible and fantastic in every area. Find support in the media you choose, the books you read, the websites you visit, the workshops you attend and the people you choose to emulate. Find role models in various areas of your life that are doing what you want to do. If you love Oprah Winfrey's ability to give, choose her as a model of the philanthropy that you choose to do. Who do you admire in the arena of business? Is Richard Branson your style, or Robert and Kim Kiyosaki? It doesn't need to be somebody famous to be effective. Your role models and mentors simply need to be people you admire in a particular area.

Brenda told me that I have been a positive influence in her life as she reads my monthly newsletters and hangs out with me whenever possible. You may be a mentor to someone and you aren't even aware that you are having a positive effect on someone's life just by being you. I personally have mentors that have never met me, such as Joyce

Meyer and Marianne Williamson. There are many things I admire about these strong female leaders as well as some things that I don't agree with, but I focus on what I wish to imitate in my own life and look for other role models in the areas that I don't. So look for friends, role models and mentors who will give you a broad range of qualities and attributes that mean something to you.

Also work on being the kind of friend whom others want to have in their life. If you don't have a lot of friends or people who want to be your friend, then really look at what kind of emotional support you provide and notice how positive or negative you are in your daily speech and conduct. Something really important in this area is that the greater my own level of self-esteem is, the easier it is to celebrate other's victories. So be aware of when you judge, criticize or feel envy around someone else's successes. Then ask yourself what it is about what they are doing that you really want to do. If you are jealous of me traveling the world for example, then maybe you are harboring a really strong desire to travel and you have suppressed it because of uncovered fears, doubts or guilt you have been afraid to express.

Those negative emotions *can* have a positive effect—they let us know where we are unhappy or dissatisfied with life. If I feel envy over someone's great figure, I know it's because I'm not as happy as I could be with my present body condition. It brings to the forefront an obviously strong desire to get more fit. If you are critical of a person's wealth, take it as a big clue that you are pissed off with your own financial situation. It's never about the other person—they are just a perfect mirror of what we would like in our own life. So celebrate that you can now recognize that sarcasm, cattiness or bitchiness surfacing in you, not as something to judge or beat yourself up over, but as something to notice and be aware of. Thank your team for bringing a desire, goal or dream to your attention and an area where you want to make some changes.

Doesn't that feel much better than beating yourself up? You're getting it!

Chapter Thirty-Three...

When it comes to leaving the merry-go-round of life in a developed country, the Sacred Gift of Extraordinary Trust is one that you may or may not have.

Extraordinary trust is when you just know it's going to work out. You don't need the tour bus; it doesn't need to be all mapped out; your ducks don't need to be lined up in a row. You thrive on the uncertainty. You just KNOW that it will all work out somehow, some way. It always does. It always will. If you have that Sacred Gift, making a move like this will be easier for you. Plain and simple.

When I decided to move to Mexico, it was on the spur-of-the-moment. My landlords were selling my condo, and I wasn't enjoying having people traipse through my condo constantly, opening up closets and snooping through cupboards. Greg and I were planning a trip to Mazatlán for a two-week vacation, and I simply decided I would stay. I literally had just forty days to sell everything, put what I wanted to keep in storage, and get organized to leave. But January 1st I arrived in Mazatlán and I knew that I had two weeks to have a vacation with Greg AND find a place to live.

Thank goodness, my friends never thought I was crazy, although I am sure they rolled their eyes a few times when I wasn't looking. I know that Greg was a bit nervous leaving me behind in Mazatlán and was very committed to my finding a safe and suitable home. But in my mind, it was a done deal. In my mind, my ability to speak fluent Spanish would suffice for me to find a place to live. I had lived in Ecuador for four years from 1991 to 1995 and therefore was confident I would adjust easily to life in Mexico with all of its modern amenities. Believe me—this is a piece of cake compared to life in Ecuador sixteen years ago!

It simply never entered my mind that I was coming into a top tourist destination at peak season and that I would be homeless on the 15th of January. My Sacred Gift of Extraordinary Trust kicked in big time, and it felt as natural to me as going out on Saturday night in Vancouver with no dinner reservations. My furniture was sold, my condo was no longer available to me, and my mail was being forwarded to my sister. Failure was simply not an option. How could it be? I needed a home in Mazatlán for a minimum of six months and I would surely find it.

Now if this sounds like you, you probably have the Sacred Gift of Extraordinary Trust. If on the other hand you are freaking out and feeling slightly queasy at just the thought of arriving in a strange city with two suitcases and nowhere to live, then you probably don't—and that's okay too. I understand that many people will need far more security than I do and will want more ducks lined up in a row than I need. Just know that about yourself and plan accordingly. It's not right or wrong—it's as much a natural way of living as it is for someone with the Gift of Music to sit down and compose a song in fifteen minutes or for someone with the Gift of Hospitality to host a dinner for 150 people without blinking an eye.

So if you read a book like Timothy Ferriss's *The 4-Hour Work Week* and can't imagine yourself jetting around the world with no agenda, no structure and no plans because you don't have that level of trust, know that you can still have a wonderful lifestyle in a developing country. You will just need to plan more, know more, research more and risk less to be comfortable. Once you get over the idea that you have to do it like Timothy Ferriss, Elizabeth Gilbert (author of *Eat, Pray, Love*) or Jan Janzen, you will have found your way off the big merry-go-round of "there is only one way to do this" thinking. If radical trust ain't your cup of tea, order a different cup of tea.

Remember it's all about choice. So simply choose differently, but know that you can still choose.

Chapter Thirty-Four...

Another important thing to remember as you choose a new lifestyle in a different country is that things *will* be different. You are not going to be able to completely transfer home to another country even if you decide to ship furniture and personal belongings halfway around the world. Having the ability to adapt, be flexible and realize that you are a guest in another country will go a long way to creating a stress-free life.

We moved to Ecuador in the midst of my not-so-nice days, and I still recall exploding over a glass tabletop that we had custom-made. I wanted it to be round, just like the one I had sold at home before moving to Ecuador. When we went to pick it up from the glass cutters, the edges were uneven and jagged. In my extremely limited Spanish, between my tears of frustration, disgust and horror, I made my disappointment obvious. Those poor workers must have thought I was a bitch from hell. They had done their best with limited tools, and I tore a strip off of them. It was not a pretty sight.

We didn't keep that table for long. Expecting what I had left behind to be recreated in Ecuador in 1991 in the small city of Quevedo was asking for a miracle, but I didn't appreciate that. I can look back and recognize what I sometimes see in tourists visiting Mexico. They complain loudly when the food isn't what they expected, the weather isn't what they were hoping for, or the service is slow and undependable. If you are thinking about making a lifestyle change, look at your ability to be flexible, adaptable and forgiving.

I fell flat on my face a few weeks after arriving in Mazatlán as I walked into a new grocery store. Intent on locating the shopping carts, I missed the fact that the pavement was intentionally uneven and very quickly found myself sprawled most ungracefully in front of a lot of people. I could have blamed the stupid grocery store for having built such a ridiculously dangerous sidewalk, but what was the point? I got up, brushed myself off, and did my shopping. A few years ago, I know that I would have demanded to see the manager and made quite a fuss. So look at yourself and ascertain now whether or not change is something you handle well or not. The belief that you must be in control, that there is only one way to do something and that it is YOUR way, and the need for everything to be perfect will be beliefs that take away much of your joy living in a foreign country. If lousy drivers, incompetent service, and out-of-service machines drive you crazy at home, what do you expect to change when you live or travel in another country?

Life in another country is one of the most invigorating choices you can make. Let me tell you, I have NO desire to return to life in the North. None! I'll visit. I'll return to do speaking engagements. But I am hooked on an easier-going attitude, a slower pace, blue skies and lots of sunshine as my daily diet. There are people who could live here and be miserable, find fault, pick apart, become a victim and complain despite the friendly people, great weather and beautiful scenery. But those people are people who are miserable anywhere. The geography does not change you—only you can do that, so start now by releasing the beliefs that cause you stress, fear, doubt and guilt.

 **Ask Yourself:**

- How flexible and adaptable am I in my life now?

- What bugs me when I travel?

- How much do I complain about where I currently live?

Chapter Thirty-Five...

What about the guilt? Interestingly, as I was preparing to move here, one of the first questions I would hear was, "What about your boyfriend?" My response was always, "What *about* my boyfriend?"

People assumed I should feel guilty or bad about moving to Mexico when my partner was still living in Seattle. Really? I guess I could feel guilty about leaving an 85-year-old father in B.C., my boyfriend in Seattle, my best friend in Vancouver, and a host of other things, but guilt is really exhausting—have you noticed? I lived on guilt for 38 years, fed it morning, noon and night, and it doesn't feel good anymore. Guilt is corrosive—it eats away at us like the rust on an anchor left in saltwater.

So how do you let go of guilt? Guilt comes from a number of beliefs. One is the familiar one: People won't like me if I do what I want. In fact, Greg loves me even more for having the courage to do what I wanted. He is making plans to join me and is bringing along his 96-year-old mother, who is so excited about spending next winter in Mexico. Not everyone will like you if you stay where you are, and not everyone will like you if you move to where you want to live— so stop worrying about it and do what you want to do!

The second trigger for guilt is the Tribal Mentality belief that if we do what we want, then God or a Universal Power will punish us or something bad will happen. As children, most of us were, unfortunately, programmed to believe that if we did what we wanted—ate the cake we weren't supposed to eat, played with the kid our parents didn't approve of, read under the covers the book our parents had prohibited—then we were bad and were made to feel guilty. Most parents seem to have taken University level courses in how to make a child feel guilty. When we didn't eat all our dinner, we heard about the children starving in India. When we didn't do our homework, we heard about the fact that they walked for five miles for the privilege of going to school. When we fought over a toy, we heard about the sacrifices they made to buy it for us. I'm not blaming parents. They surely learned well from their parents—who I suppose walked 20 miles to school, in freezing cold, with no shoes on, uphill both ways—but it has programmed us to believe that if we step out of the Tribe, do what we want, deviate from the norm, we are bad and we should feel guilty. So let's let go of the belief that doing what we want makes us putty in the hands of a wicked Devil, sentenced to hell, evil, imperfect and waiting to be punished, shall we?

Living without guilt is a huge relief. Your cells will thank you for it as guilt weighs heavily on them. Just think about all the things you do because if you DIDN'T, you'd feel guilty. Perhaps it is how you dress, drive, do business, raise your children, eat, or any of a million other things. Just think about what you really want to do in your life— whether that be to live in a hot, sunny climate or travel or change your career, friends, workplace, religion, home or community—and see what guilty feelings suddenly well up in you. Then let them go because they are *probably not yours*. You were "gifted" them from Mom, Dad, grandparents, religious leaders, teachers, media and your culture. The minute I feel that I "should" do something out of guilt, I stop and decide whether it is a "should" that I want to become a conscious choice, or something I can let go the way of the dodo bird. Most of the time, I can let it go. In the rare case where I really do want to keep it, making it a conscious choice changes the vibration around it and it feels a thousand times better just by making that choice.

Chapter Thirty-Six...

It's so easy to put off doing what we want to do. People know they procrastinate and they hate it—and then they continue to do it. I actually don't believe there is such a thing as procrastination. The dictionary defines procrastination as "postponing or delaying needlessly."

There are three reasons why you postpone or delay needlessly. One is insufficient passion to get a task done. The second is fear of what will happen if you actually take action and get something done. Third, it may really not be the right time to do something and you are being directed by your soul to wait. So let's forget about calling procrastination the problem. It is simply the symptom of these three issues.

Let's say that you want to take your business to the next level of success because you are tired of being on the merry-go-round of "not enough money." You know you should do more marketing. You agree you should be contacting your clients. You realize a more aggressive public relations campaign would grow your business. But you look at the marketing options and you can't decide. You go to pick up the phone to contact a client—then you put it down and make yourself a coffee instead. You meet with a PR firm and make the excuse that you just don't have the money. This may apply to renovating your house, starting a business, fixing your marriage, writing a book or a host of other things on your To-Do list for life. But you just can't do what it takes to make it happen.

Ask yourself this question: How PASSIONATE am I about doing this? If you are trying to build a business that you don't really like, your passion level on a scale of 1 to 10 is probably about a 2. If you are trying to renovate a home that you would rather sell, then your passion level may be hovering at a 1. So how passionate are you about what is on your To-Do List for life? Maybe everybody has told you that you should write a book because you tell such great stories. But as much as you like telling the stories, you have no passion to sit down and write, so your passion for actually writing a book is extremely low. Just acknowledging your passion level about what you are procrastinating about will give you a big clue as to why the task is not getting done.

If you really love to write and your passion is at a 10 to write a book but it's still not getting done, then ask yourself: What am I afraid will happen if I write this book? Perhaps you are afraid that no one will read the book. Maybe you are afraid of all the things that you don't know how to do—find a publisher or self-publish, find an editor, find an illustrator and a printer. What would change in your life if all of sudden it was a bestseller and you found yourself on Oprah's Book Club list? Yikes, how would massive fame and notoriety change your quiet, private, sheltered life in rural Ohio? Those are good questions to think about.

If you are putting off getting out of a marriage that is no longer working, then what fears are you facing? It's very normal to be afraid of life after marriage, especially if you have been married for many years. That's a good reason to procrastinate and not ask for the divorce. Most people who have ended a marriage would tell you that it's difficult to get out in the world again, by yourself, or to start dating again at 40, 50, or older. That's a big fear. There's definitely some-thing to the saying, "The devil you know is better than the devil you don't." At least you know the mate you're living with, and you don't know who you will end up with once that marriage is over with, or if there even will be another partner. That's enough to scare you into complacency and procrastination.

You can do this with every event in your life that you believe you are procrastinating over. Make a list of what you believe you are postponing or delaying needlessly. Then ask yourself: What is my level of passion around this? Secondly, ask yourself, what am I afraid of around this subject? If you don't get answers on either of those questions—and that is possible—consider the possibility that you are being directly guided to wait. "Timing is everything" is a very popular saying, but we don't seem to pay much heed to that saying in our own life.

How high is the quality of patience on your personal value scale? We live in a "have it now," immediate gratification society that is focused on the present. Buy now, pay later is the predominant theme of marketing campaigns. So it can be hard to want something now, to have it on our wish list, our intention list or on our To-Do list, but every time we go to do it, we get pulled off track, delayed or postponed in what looks to us as procrastination.

Perhaps there really is a Higher Power that is working with us at a soul level that is delaying things for a very good reason. Maybe the ideal partner is still healing from a past relationship and isn't quite ready for you to enter his life. Have you considered the possibility that the market isn't primed yet for your new product because there is something that needs to come before it that will really set it off? I know if I had decided to launch a pole dancing business in 1995, it probably wouldn't have been much of a success. But launching it in 2004 was another matter, when everyone from Barbara Walters to Oprah Winfrey was talking about pole dancing and had even pole danced live on television! So trust that you may be delayed, postponed or held back from moving forward at your desired speed of things for good reason. Is procrastination a problem? No, but lack of passion, fear and Divine timing are issues that can masquerade as procrastination.

Remove the word from your vocabulary and start looking at the real issues behind what the Tribe calls "procrastination."

Chapter Thirty-seven...

Diane loved the merry-go-round of inaction. She just wouldn't move forward. In a healing session, we identified it as the syndrome of anticipatory-versus-participatory. What does that mean? If you are always in a state of anticipation, planning, waiting and expecting things, it's a very safe feeling. Anticipating the flight, the relationship, or the workshop you really want to teach is a very, very safe place to be. Participating in the activity, flying, getting along with someone or actually teaching the workshop is quite different. Now things can go wrong. The plane can crash, you can find out you're not as easy to get along with as you thought and people don't actually want to attend your workshop. Yes, being in surgery is considerably riskier than being in the waiting room.

So you will hang on to the excuses that it's not yet perfect, things haven't lined up yet, you're still deciding, it's all up in the air, it's manifesting, and a host of other excuses which keep you in the "anticipatory" state. But if you never move out of that state, you lose out on a tremendous amount of success, joy, peace, love and prosperity.

All of us have met the person who is always in the planning stage. Every time you meet them, they are planning to sell their house or start that business or move to another country. It's always in the future. They simply never take action. That syndrome of anticipatory-versus-participatory is based on several common beliefs:

1. You may fail if you take action and all of the fear, doubt, guilt and shame about failing shows up pretty darn quickly.

2. You will now be responsible for what you do. Many people have a huge resentment towards responsibility because they were expected to help raise their younger siblings, help out

around the house, feed the chickens, milk the cows and a host of other chores, oftentimes at very young ages. There is a resentment towards responsibility. This level of responsibility also triggers a fear of not doing it right, or well or perfectly and disappointing parents, partners, siblings, employees, friends, and perhaps most importantly themselves.

3. You may actually succeed and that is uncomfortable. Failure is usually more comfortable than success because you feel like you know it more intimately.

4. If you actually do what you plan on doing, then what next? What will really happen after that? That's a big unanswered question that isn't always comfortable either. So acknowledge and release these worries, concerns, doubts and fears and move into full participation in life. It's way more fun to be "in" the game than sitting on the sidelines. It's much more exhilarating to be "in" the plane going somewhere exciting than sitting in the waiting room at the airport waving good-bye as the plane leaves. Notice where you are always in an anticipatory emotion in your life rather than a participatory one and decide today to take action.

          Getting Off the Merry-Go-Round

Chapter Thirty-Eight...

It may be really comfortable on the merry-go-round of fear, doubt and guilt. It's like an old sweater that has definitely seen better days and smelled sweeter, but you just don't want to part with it.

Some of us really like playing the victim, having a "story" to tell, living the soap opera drama. It gets us attention, is our trademark, and makes up our identity.

How about you? Do you like the drama? Are you happy playing the victim? I remember my mom heading out to a party one evening several years ago. It was a few years after her divorce, which had followed 47 years of marriage. Mom was having a hard time adjusting to life on her own, yet she also loved her new-found freedom. The problem was this: as far back as I could remember, Mom was usually sick. That night, as I knew she was headed out to a social event, I suggested she take some more of the algae capsules that had been making her feel better. She looked at me and said, "But then who would know that I'm sick?"

Ouch! That one hit me like a slap across the face. Did she really mean it? Unfortunately, my mother, so accustomed to her story, her drama, her victimhood of being sick, was quite uncomfortable and even fearful of letting go. It was her security blanket, her way out of difficult situations, her answer when she didn't want to do something.

I empathized with her because I had been on a similar path. In my 30s, suffering with various ailments from life in Ecuador, struggling with depression and at times suicidal, I had a great excuse anytime I didn't want to step up or step out. But I recognized at the time that the syndrome I had seen for years in my mother was showing up in myself. I knew I really had to stop that merry-go-round, get off and walk away from being the victim. Once in awhile I slipped back.

Particularly when going through times of financial hardship, it was easy to get out the violin and start playing the same tune. One day though, a very dear friend looked at me and said, "When are you going to give up the story, Jan?"

I stopped, stunned and speechless. She was right—so right it stung. I was playing the victim again, with all of the expertise of a professional.

So are you a professional victim? Do you like that merry-go-round of drama, chaos, and old stories of oppression, persecution and catastrophe? If so, you will find it most challenging to live a life full of joy, peace, love and prosperity because the two do not go hand-in-hand. Ever. Retelling old accounts of people who did you wrong, rehashing old sicknesses and accidents and recounting stories of financial woes will keep telling the Subconscious Mind, "This is important. Keep these files prominent and handy for future reference."

Why are some people such great victims? It's like they relish the pain and suffering. There are very likely some old files that look like this: "You need to suffer to be good. Good people suffer, wicked people prosper. If I'm not sick, I don't get any attention. Nobody loves me, hugs me, or kisses me when I'm healthy, so I need to be sick." Do you see how old beliefs will fuel the fire of victimhood?

So if you would win the Academy Award for Victim of the Year, ask yourself why you enjoy being the victim. What is it about the drama, the victimhood, the pain and the struggling that you believe you need to hang on to? If you think you need to be crucified to be seen as good, godly or righteous, then you will sabotage yourself every time. Why wouldn't you? If your Subconscious Mind links suffering and pain to being "good enough," "saved," "righteous," and "spiritual," then you will do a mighty fine job. Look carefully at what the motive is behind you playing victim and decide whether or not you are ready to let it go.

Ask Yourself:

Do I:

- Retell old stories that are negative?
- Complain about the past?
- Regret the past?
- Relish the drama?
- Nurture the chaos?

If it's hard to be honest on this one, simply ask your friends and ask them to be honest and open with you.

Chapter Thirty-Nine...

One of the most common Tribal Mentality beliefs is that life is a rollercoaster—there's good and bad and everything in between. So we live in expectation of the bad and not so great. After describing a good thing, you'll hear people say, "Knock on wood," which they think ensures that the good thing will hang in there for longer. Or they'll say things like, "You've got to take the bad with the good." And they are absolutely right in one way: If that's what they believe, it will come true.

There are two things about this belief. One is that defining something as "good" or "bad" is really more about perspective than anything. Let's say that someone threw a bucket of water on four different people. One person may rant and rave about their ruined clothes and spoilt hairdo and talk about that bucket of water for days or weeks with a lot of anger and negative emotion. The next person may just think the whole thing was silly, go change their clothes and not give it much thought. The third person could think it was fabulous as they were so hot and this was just what they needed so they may actually feel gratitude. The fourth may think "What fun!" and join in, making it a massive water fight, laughing and playing with the buckets of water.

Haven't you seen that happen with many different things in life? I might feel that noisy kids yelling in the pool is annoying, while Grandma thinks they're adorable and loves watching them play. I can think my place is gorgeous, but a multi-millionaire may think it's small and ugly. It all comes down to perspective. Nothing in life has a story until we bring our story to it. Remember that because it is critical to creating a magnificent life. Nothing in life has a story until we bring our story to it.

So back to good versus bad. Life happens. Period. It is much more about HOW we view life than WHAT actually happens. So are there good and bad things that happen? Of course. I'm sure that lots of bad things happen to me just like they happen to you. I just don't see many things in life as bad. If I don't like the grandkids yelling in the pool, then I can choose to go sit in the sun where it's quieter or go for a swim in the ocean. If someone does something to me that isn't nice, I have the choice to get upset or to laugh it off and forget it. So believing that life is a rollercoaster of good and bad and that we need to expect the "bad" has a lot to do with perspective.

I saw this recently while doing a tour of some of the poorer areas of Mazatlán. I was on a local church tour helping to feed some of the poorest workers in the city when I had the privilege of meeting Gloria. Gloria is a grandmother with more than 30 grandchildren of her own. She lives in a hovel, and that's really stretching it. It was one of the worst homes I have ever seen, and I've travelled through many developing countries. Chickens, pigs, and rabbits make their home with Gloria. There was dirt everywhere and the smell was overwhelmingly horrid. The kitchen was in shambles and I never saw anything that even resembled a bathroom. (You can see pictures of Gloria's home on my website at www.janjanzen.com/gallery.htm) Yet Gloria showed us through her home like she was guiding us through the Taj Mahal. It was fascinating to watch her stand in the middle of her empire like the empress herself.

To Gloria, this was good. To the rest of us, this was abysmal. Same house, same issues, but very different perspectives. So one major antidote to the good/bad/good/bad rollercoaster of life is to appreciate that your definition of bad and good is simply your perspective and that it can be easily changed.

Let's look at another way of overcoming this belief that there needs to be bad following the good.

Ask Yourself:

- What "story" do I consistently bring to life?

- Is it positive or negative?

- What is the new perspective I choose to bring to life?

Chapter Forty...

Many people think we need the bad or the negative to appreciate the good or the positive. I disagree. At this age in my life—closer to 50 than 40—I've been through some bad things like all of us. Do we really need more bad things to appreciate the good? I don't think so. I do not need to lose my eyesight to appreciate the sunset off my balcony every night. Do you need to go without food to know how much you enjoy eating? Hardly. And we certainly don't need to experience pain to know that we don't like it.

Every one of us has experienced bad things in this lifetime and every other life we have ever lived. So this is my argument in the Universal Court: I promise to appreciate the good, be grateful for the amazing, and truly love my life. In return, I'll take the good, lots of good, all good, for the rest of my days, thank you very much. I promise to not take it for granted but to appreciate what I have, use it in service to others and come from a place of gratitude daily. In exchange, bring on more good, God. I expect it, I anticipate it, and I live in an eager excitement about all the good things that are coming.

I'm serious. Rather than wait for the shoe to drop, the bottom to fall out, and the you-know-what to hit the fans, why not get up every morning excited about the good things coming your way? How about waiting like a child on Christmas morning to see what goodness is in store for you? It's just a matter of attitude, perspective and focus.

My dearest friend Monique says that I have a radical relationship with God. Maybe I do. To me, it seems pretty normal to expect amazing things from the Universe. I do my best to be a good person, help others, really listen to the instructions that come from above and within, and work on myself to always improve. I think that deserves rewarding, I really do. Maybe that's why I feel like my life flows in a most magnificent way. I love the twists and turns, the surprises and the excitement. I say to God almost every day, "I don't know what you have planned for me today God, but I KNOW it's good," and then I wait for the good things to happen. Expect the worst possible scenario and you probably won't be in for peaches and cream. I don't expect just any old peaches and cream, but the best peaches and cream AND a cherry on top! In other words, I expect the best. Why wouldn't I? Why wouldn't you?

Let's find out.

Chapter Forty-One...

M any people expect bad things to happen to them because "that's just life." It's the way it's always been and is, and so they think, "Why would I get anything different than the rest of humanity?" That's a big Tribal Mentality belief.

Let's get rid of it, shall we?

That belief stems from the core of "I'm not okay, I'm not good enough and I'm bad." Did you know that by the time a child is five years old, he has heard the word "No" an estimated 60,000 times? How many times have we heard that we are bad, wicked, evil, wrong, imperfect, screwed up, stupid, foolish and a host of other even more demeaning things over the years? Some of my clients have been called names by their parents that would make a sailor blush. Parents, teachers, siblings, friends, employers and religious leaders have all contributed to the belief in us that we don't do much right.

My parents called me The Mistake for the first six years of my life because I wasn't a planned pregnancy. How many babies out there really were? Not many, from what I can tell. And some parents, even in jest, reinforced the belief that we weren't really wanted. My religious upbringing drilled into my little heart and head that it was only by the UNDESERVED sacrifice of Jesus Christ that I could be saved. I was a condemned sinner, wicked to the core and grossly imperfect. Those are not particularly empowering words by anybody's standards. Yet they were indoctrinated into me, morning, noon and night for 38 years as they are in many religions. Need we wonder why people's self-esteem is so incredibly low when these ideas are being promulgated by some of the most powerful religions in the world?

Let's face it—according to the Tribe, we don't do much right. That's the whole point of the Tribe. If you're never good enough, if you never develop any self-confidence or personal power, then you don't leave.

You put up with the fear-mongering and humiliating belief systems and accept it as normal. I mean, what's your choice? Leaving the Tribe is a scary prospect, or so they make it seem. Every time I go through the security systems at the airport and have to take off my shoes and my belt, and can't have a toothpaste tube with me or nail clippers, I am uneasily aware of the fear that the Tribe is instilling in us daily. Each magazine I flip through with advertisements for the latest wrinkle removal technique or the newest weight loss product is more affirmation that you aren't good enough, skinny enough, smart enough, rich enough or anything else enough.

One of the fastest growing areas in the cosmetic surgery arena is labia and vaginal surgery because women's labia and vaginas just aren't good enough anymore! They're not tight enough, small enough, nor pert enough. Good God! Where does the insanity stop? We already know my hips aren't right, my breasts aren't perfect, my lips aren't okay—so what comes after my labia? If all the advertising that hits my email inbox daily is any indication, there isn't a man out there with the right size penis, either. So I guess my labia is fair game after all!

By the time we get through all the pervasive media and our own internal belief system that has been programmed since infancy, of course you would expect bad things in your life. If you're bad, through and through, how much good can you really expect to happen to you?

Let go of the beliefs right now that you aren't okay, not good enough, undeserving, wicked, evil, a sinner and any other nasty thing that comes up for you. The sooner you realize that you are amazing just the way you are, the closer you are to achieving a life that is joyful, peaceful, loving and abundant. So let's begin right now, shall we?

Chapter Forty-Two...

I may have hit on a raw nerve if you consider yourself a religious person. First of all, let me clarify something. I was a religious person for most of my life. What I learned after leaving the religion of my upbringing is that religious and spiritual are two very different ideas.

When we lived in Ecuador as missionaries, we were surrounded by Catholics. Many were very responsive to our message but we were also robbed seven times in four years. We lived in a walled yard with bars on our windows and an alarm system. Our vehicle had to be inside the walls every night (you never see a car parked on the street at night in Ecuador). As we went from door to door and heard that these people believed the Bible also, my next question would be: "If that is so, why have I been robbed seven times in four years?" It really was an innocent question because I had had it drilled into me that as a religious person, I didn't steal.

Many people confuse being religious with being spiritual. Sometimes they do cross over. Other times, being involved in a certain religion is more of a label or part of a culture. This would appear to be the case in Ecuador, for example. However, many of those strong religious beliefs have become an intrinsic part of who we are. Fear and guilt were certainly indoctrinated in me daily and became part of my psyche—fear of impending doom, fear of not being worthy, of not staying on the straight and narrow, of the Devil tempting me, of God testing me, and on and on and on. The Devil was in the movies, books, a skirt above my knees and a top that showed any cleavage. I learned to walk around like the Devil was a roaring lion waiting to get me!

Living with such fear is neither healthy nor particularly fun. It also takes away a tremendous amount of our power. Why do I say that? Because either the Devil is tempting us or God is testing us, so we're hooped no matter what. That belief has you coming and going. Responsibility is absolutely impossible with both good and evil out to get you. With the feeling of choice, responsibility, and power removed, we feel vulnerable and helpless—exactly where religion would like us to be. It can thoroughly perpetrate that feeling of victimhood, complete with all the drama. I've watched people live their lives as if they were nailed to a cross and saving the world. I suggest you get off the cross and burn it. Live life fully because if indeed Jesus did die for us, then it's been done, once and for all, and you don't need to be the second Messiah!

Then there is the guilt—guilt around sinning, guilt around not being good enough, being undeserving, or having evil thoughts. Guilt is a heavy emotion to deal with, and religion uses it extensively with teachings of hell, purgatory and other such beliefs. Even the belief that we needed to be saved, that someone needed to suffer and die to buy us back through a ransom sacrifice puts a level of guilt on us that is unbearable.

In his book *The God Code*, Gregg Braden writes that in his scientific studies, he has discovered that written in the very DNA of our cells are the words, God/Eternal within the Body. That is very powerful. Does that mean at the very core of who we are, at the very essence of our being, in our DNA, that we are divine, a child of God and perfect? I believe so. All disempowering beliefs are like layers of ugly wallpaper on a beautiful mahogany wall. The wall never disappears, it just gets hidden under all of the paper. Likewise, in the very core of our DNA we are divine, but that divinity gets buried under all the human stuff that languishes in the fear, doubt and guilt. So let's release at a DNA and cellular level the negative emotions around not being good enough, being a sinner, imperfect, and evil and bask in the knowledge that you are perfect, divine, a child of God and absolutely incredible. Feel that to your very core.

It feels pretty darn good, doesn't it?

Chapter Forty-Three...

Let's talk about the other topic we're not supposed to talk about—you know the word that is searched more than any other word on the Internet and no, it's not vacations. It's sex. That's an interesting merry-go-round now isn't it? Should you or shouldn't you? Do you enjoy it or pretend you don't? When do you do it, how do you do it and why do you do it?

There are a lot of Tribal Mentality beliefs around sex, genetic coding around sex, beliefs we adopted from Mom and Dad around sex (although of course they never did it—except maybe once). We carry a lot of little packs on our cells around sex. So how do they affect us? Sex comes up a lot in sessions with my clients, because although we aren't really supposed to talk about it, it's there in our face, constantly.

Unfortunately, we have had many conflicting programs instilled in us. As women, we are supposed to be virginal and pure until we meet the man we want to marry, and then we're supposed to know how to be the seductress and temptress—all automatically of course. Men aren't quite sure what to do these days with women either, and it's causing friction and lots of it. People assume that married people are getting sex and single people aren't, but that's certainly not true. I have worked with married couples who haven't had sex in months or years. Our parents brought a lot of baggage to us around this topic, as oftentimes they were raised by parents who never talked about sex, ever. Everybody **automatically** assumes that we'll just figure it out somehow, someway. But the fact that sex is a major reason for marital discord, that we have epidemics of teenage pregnancies, and that rape is a common practice in every country in the world leads me to say we haven't done a great job of automatically figuring it out.

Religion has contributed greatly to the problem, adding lots of guilt, fear and doubt to the melting pot of already conflicting viewpoints. So let's release some of the unhelpful beliefs around sex, shall we? Let go of the belief that sex is dirty, wicked, unscriptural, painful, selfish and controlling. Let's release at a DNA and cellular level the idea that sex is something God frowns upon. And let's replace those beliefs with healthy beliefs around sex—that it is a gift to humans, a beautiful expression of love, an honor to be intimate with someone, and something respectful, loving, kind, generous and joyful. Know in every cell of your body that sex is something God created and purposed for our enjoyment.

In order to accept that sex is pleasurable and that you can enjoy it respectfully with peace, love and joy, look at your own ideas around sex to see where you are blocked. We have all had past lives where sex has been used as a weapon against us, used to manipulate us, overpower us and control us. That is all in the past—today is a new day to embrace a more loving and honoring view of sex.

Chapter Forty-Four...

Is there really such a thing as past lives? That's a good question. I don't know that we'll ever have the definitive answer on that one. What I do know is many things that were unsolvable or unexplainable **without** believing in past lives were solved and healed through acceptance of the idea of past lives.

Every time I sat down to write my first book, I would have strange pains running down my arms. If it had only been the left arm, I would have thought I was having a heart attack. But it felt like there was a pinched nerve in each of my armpits, resulting in these numbing sensations down the arms. It didn't stop me from writing but it certainly made it uncomfortable. One day I got a very clear visual of a person pinned to a flat rocklike surface with his arms tied down with chains that went under his armpits. The sun was hot and the man was obviously dying a very painful and slow death. The story I got with the visual was that I had been a subversive writer and was dying for my writing. I healed and let go of the memory and the pains vanished.

I finished my provocative and controversial book, *Devil with a Briefcase*, and have never had the pain again. Coincidence—or past life memory? I can't tell you for sure. I can only tell you the results.

One of my clients phoned for her appointment, and immediately after I asked how she was doing, she burst into tears. I found out that one of her twins, a 3½-year-old boy, screamed constantly. He was now falling behind seriously in his speech development and his twin brother was far ahead of him in speaking capabilities. Besides not being great for learning to speak, the screaming was driving his mother absolutely crazy.

I tapped into her young son, and what I saw instantly was a person being burned alive at a stake. The flames were coming up and burning his flesh and he was—you guessed it—screaming. I did some healing work on Jonathan, and yup, you guessed again, the screaming stopped.

Today, Jonathan is catching up nicely on his speech development. That Christmas, I got the most beautiful email from my client thanking me for the peace that I had brought to the family.

So do past lives really have an effect on our lives today? I believe after working with hundreds and hundreds of past life stories, the answer is yes. Let me explain why.

Past lives or reincarnation is a belief of many religions and spiritual movements. From early times in India to ancient Greek philosophers to modern day New Age movements, a belief that we have had past lives is popular. This belief states that as we reincarnate, we do so in a different body. What do you believe?

Chapter Forty-Five...

If your soul has indeed lived a number of lives, then every lifetime has memories, just like the current one. I believe these soul memories are stored in the Subconscious Mind along with every memory from this life. So just as I mentioned previously that negative files often get the most charge in our lives and the Subconscious Mind files those incidents with special red flags that say, "Pay attention to me," then a negative incident from a past life can very much be affecting you today. I have seen this in working with married couples. If they are having challenges in this life, they are often reliving a past life together where they may have been married, siblings, business partners or lovers. By clearing the negative emotions from the past life or lives, this life can change dramatically. We really do hang out with a pretty small group of souls. One time you're Mom, the next time I am, the next time I'm Dad, and so on and so on. One of my clients had a best friend who was totally controlling. She was manipulative and conniving, demanding and really witchy. When I checked in, she had been my client's mother in another lifetime and she came back to this one with a similar agenda.

My current partner in life and I have spent many lifetimes as husband and wife and have had some great times together. We have an almost magical relationship built on deep respect, and a profound mutual understanding, which came very early on in this lifetime's relationship. Someone who absolutely drives you crazy may have been an abusive parent, a cheating business partner or a manipulative sibling in another lifetime.

You can dismiss this whole concept as absurd or impossible, unscriptural or wrong, and that's fine with me. I just looked for results, and I definitely got and continue to get great results with the past life work that I do.

Chapter Forty-Six...

Can we really change those past life memories and emotions? Yes we can. It's all about releasing and letting go of the files and all of the emotions related to them. Many spiritual practitioners and workshop facilitators talk about releasing the memory, but I have found in my own personal experience and in working through well over a thousand sessions with clients that the emotions related to that memory must be released as well.

Remember my story of the emotion of fear that holds you back from looking over the edge of a balcony? You can remove a memory of falling from a high place, but it is the emotion *attached* to that memory that is stopping you from being able to lean over. The feeling of terror and lack of control will be the emotions that need to be released as well. That memory has no charge without the emotion.

If I tell you about a cabin in the woods on the ocean, you may picture a cute little cabin from a movie you once saw or a resort you once visited. Immediately there will be an emotion associated with that memory. If I mentioned Port Shepstone, South Africa and you have never been there or seen pictures of it, there is no memory or emotion. Memory PLUS emotion go hand-in-hand. You try to pull up a memory without having an emotion tied to it and it is impossible. So from a healing and clearing point of view, releasing a memory without releasing the attached emotions is impossible. One of the ways to see what file you have linked to anything is to say a word and then see what immediately comes up after it. If I say SEX to you, what comes up for you? Fun, pleasure, fear, pain, dirty, immoral—or something else? If I say MONEY to you, what immediately comes up? Hard to get, difficult, not enough, plenty, abundance, dirty, denied—or another word? By seeing what files are linked to important things in your life, you can start to understand why you do what you do and why you create the results you create.

For example, if sex brings up the link to pain, then how much are you going to want sex? Probably not much, unless of course you have a good association to pain, which is sometimes the case. If money brings up the association of "hard to get," then every time you think about money, "hard to get" comes up immediately, and it's what you create. This exercise can be most revealing. Words are thoughts expressed, so every time you speak about sex, men, women, money, marriage, living on a beach in Tahiti, or growing your business, just note what words and emotions are associated with it.

Many clients can't figure out why they aren't in a relationship and then I discover that their association with the word "men" is "untrustworthy, unreliable, sloppy, heartbreakers," and a host of other nasty words. It's not likely that Prince Charming is going to come into their life anytime soon. But what do past lives have to do with this? Plenty. Many clients are well aware of their current beliefs. Usually by the time they come to see me, they have been through many other healers, counselors, and workshops, so they are fairly enlightened about who they are. They come to me for the stuff they still can't unearth. So they may be aware of the belief that money is hard to come by because of their upbringing by parents who struggled to put food on their table. However, if an association or file is coming from a past life that they are not aware of, then digging deeper for this file is critical.

One of my clients had a business she wanted to grow. She was doing everything but it still felt stalled. In a past life she had been a very prominent business owner and had a factory which employed many people. Much to the horror of the owner, employees, and community, that factory burnt down. The ensuing guilt and hardship were overwhelming. The understandable association in her file for building a business included hardship, guilt, fear, worry, anxiety and doubt as to its success. Interestingly she had watched a movie at one point that she vividly remembered had a similar story line. She had bawled through the movie, quite unsure of why her reaction was so severe.

Do you see how a past life experience could possibly explain certain things in your life?

Chapter Forty-Seven...

It's all about choice. You have choice. Just decide. You're creating your life. You're manifesting all of this, so just change your thoughts. Perhaps you have heard those words over and over again until you want to vomit because the last thing you feel you have is choice. You have three kids in high school. You have a father with dementia and a mother in a wheelchair. Your husband has a full-time job that seems to be constantly on the line with all the cutbacks, and you are building your own business, which is struggling because there never seems to be enough time to really sink your teeth into it. Where is the choice, and how do YOU create a life you really want without fear, doubt and guilt being what you eat for breakfast, lunch and dinner?

The first thing I want you to do is to stop and breathe. That may sound ridiculous, but let's get some Spirit flowing through you and then let's work this out.

I will always tell you that you have choice, but sometimes the biggest choice you have is in your perspective of a situation. Remember Gloria with the horrible shack in Mexico? Her perspective was incredibly positive despite the horrific situation she was in. On the other hand, how fortunate that Gloria lives in a peaceful country where starvation is rare and the weather is beautiful! Gloria actually has a lot to be grateful for, and she knows it. It's much easier to be poor when the sun shines every day and there is a warm breeze and blue sky, a papaya to pick off the tree in your front yard and an ocean full of fish at your doorstep. All you may have to change is your level of gratitude for what you really do have.

People talk about gratitude all the time, but I really believe people can improve greatly in this area. The other day while driving back from a beautiful little mining town in the mountains, we passed a

Mexican chicken farm. The Mexican woman driving the car said, "Those poor chickens." Instantly out my mouth came the words, "but look at all the fresh air they are getting." She burst out laughing. She was thinking about how sad those chickens had it in the open air buildings laying eggs and doing whatever chickens do, but my mind immediately went to how good they had it compared to chickens in the North who probably never feel a warm breeze, not even in early spring!

So what about you? You have three children in high school. How grateful you can be that they have a high school to attend, that there are teachers and supplies at that high school, and that you have three beautiful, healthy children who have lived long enough to attend school. That isn't something many people in the world take for granted or would ever complain about. You may think this is a "just think of all the starving children in India" story, but we have become incredibly apathetic about how good we have it. A wake-up call may be the very thing needed to get your life back on track.

You have parents still living! That's something to be grateful for, because once they're gone, your life will change, guaranteed. Your husband has a job! How good is that? And what a blessing that as a woman you have the opportunity where you live to exercise tremendous personal freedom and be an entrepreneur.

This may not be what you want to hear—it probably isn't—but it's absolutely correct. Look at your husband or partner and thank them for being in your life and working so hard to provide for the family. Say goodnight to each of your children and remember how precious they are. Hug your parents and tell them how grateful you are they are still in your life. Thank the one client you do have for being in your business. Start blessing. Start remembering how fortunate you are. See the glass not half full, nor half empty, but overflowing, because where there is no water, there is oxygen..

Everything around you is truly overflowing. It's a Tribal Mentality belief that life is hard, life is challenging, life is stressful. What if life were actually easy, joyful and fun? It really is. But at the same time there are challenges and stresses. Just notice where you focus, because what you focus on expands.

Can you make some changes? Probably. If the kids are not cooperating around the house, set some boundaries with repercussions. For example, nobody puts their laundry in the laundry basket and you're expected to run around and pick up dirty clothes everywhere on laundry day. Why not instead tell everyone that Friday is laundry day and laundry must be in the laundry basket on Friday morning or it won't get washed? Along comes Friday morning. There aren't a lot of clothes in the basket. What do you do? Do you run around and collect the dirty clothes? Absolutely not! What clothes are in the basket get washed, what clothes aren't don't. Let me tell you, once the kids figure out that you are serious and they have to wear dirty clothes or do their own laundry (with your permission, of course), they'll put their clothes in the basket by Friday. It's not your responsibility or worry. Let go of the belief you have to be a doormat, a slave, or the maid for everyone in your family. Let go of the belief in every cell of your body that you need to be the rescuer. When I got too demanding as a youngster, my mother used to say to me, "What happened to your slave last week? Did she die of exhaustion?" Subtle as being hit by a 2x4, but I sure remembered it when I got overzealous in ordering my mother around!

Start setting boundaries and also start communicating what you really want. Perhaps your family can take off and travel for a year. There are families with children and aged parents who have done so. Most of them weren't millionaires who just won the lotto. They have taken kids out of school, asked siblings to look after parents, taken a sabbatical from work, taken a line of credit on their house, rented it out for a year and gone backpacking through Asia for 12 months. So don't dismiss anything as being impossible. It's all possible. It really is.

One day while in the pool here in Mexico, a woman asked me what I did. As she listened to me, she wistfully said, "I want to do what you're doing." But just like Rudy, she had a list of reasons why she could not. As she explained her job to me, I started to fire back suggestions about what she could do to change her situation by thinking outside the box about her current job. Every time I said something to her, her response was the same, "I never thought about that." You may need to bounce some ideas off of a friend or coach to start brainstorming about what you really CAN do. However, if you use this principle it will be of tremendous value: Think about HOW you can do what you want rather than WHY you cannot do what you want.

Which brings me to another key point.

Ask Yourself:

- Where in your life do you feel like you don't have choice?

- How are you actually making it a choice?

- How can you look at it with a different perspective that is more empowering?

- What different choices could you make?

Example: *I sit at home alone on weekends because nobody invites me out.*

You are making it a choice because you are waiting to be invited rather than taking proactive steps. You can change your perspective by appreciating the time you have to do what you want to do and nurture yourself. You could choose to have a potluck with friends one Saturday a month, invite friends in for a board game one weekend or pursue a hobby that involves others and would keep you busy.

Chapter Forty-Eight...

How big is your WHY for creating the life you say you want?

Do you even know what your WHY is? I remember a client asking me why I was moving to Mexico. I said, "I love the lifestyle. I like taking siestas, going to the market to buy fruits and vegetables and having a more relaxed approach to life." She replied, "But you can have that here. You can go to a little vegetable market in Vancouver, you can have a nap in the afternoon if you want and you can work less and play more here, Jan." And she was absolutely right. Her comment got me really clear on what my WHY really was.

My big WHY for moving to Mexico is that I love waking up every morning to blue sky and sun. I don't even go to the vegetable market here because the grocery store has such amazing fruits and vegetables. I have rarely taken a siesta and I have been very busy with clients and projects, like writing this book, since I landed in Mexico. But what I absolutely love every single morning is opening up the curtains and smiling this great big smile because it is always blue sky and sunny. I'd live in 20 degrees below zero if it were sunny…okay, maybe not, but I certainly have done that and I loved it, because I just love the sun.

So what's your WHY? As you can tell from my reason, this doesn't have to be Plato or Einstein quality. It really doesn't. It just needs to mean something to you that is really important. After spending the last several years in Vancouver, where gray sky and rain are the normal weather pattern, I am very clear today that I want blue sky and sun as the norm in my day.

When I lived in the cabin—you know, the one in the woods with the rats—I had to have a great big WHY. It's where I learned the importance of a big WHY. I wanted privacy and solitude. I wanted to be on the ocean and in the forest. I wanted seclusion and hibernation. I wanted to be reclusive and eccentric. I really needed some serious "Jan time" to heal. So I manifested this quaint little cottage in the woods on the ocean in a regional park that was so secluded people had a terrible time finding me—but I loved it. I walked in the woods every day. I sat down on this great big rock and the ocean waves lapped up against it, teasing my toes with the cold saltwater. I sat on my porch and watched the sunsets while the kayakers were so close I could hear every word of their conversation. I built a fire for heat and sat in front of it reading and writing.

And…I lived with rats! At first, when I saw the teeth marks in the bar of soap in the bathtub at the foot of my bed, I didn't want to believe I had a mouse situation. Then I walked into the kitchen the second week there and saw a very large rodent scurrying across my countertop past my vegetables and fish that were being prepared for company. I soon realized they were running up and down my bathroom walls, having a heyday in my linens and eating my all-natural soap! When Jo, who had lived in the woods nearby for 40 years, brought me a mousetrap that would catch them alive, she showed me the hole where they entered to get the peanut butter. I still remember looking at her and saying, "Jo, anything I have seen in my cabin would not get its head into that hole. It's way too small." At which time I heard the words I never wanted to hear in my entire life: "Then, Jan, you don't have a mouse problem. You have a rat infestation."

I would walk up to the bathroom door and clap my hands a few times so they would scurry away and I could use the bathroom. I bought a mosquito net for the bed, which comforted me—until one morning I woke up and they had chewed massive holes through a thick chenille throw in the living room. So much for my flimsy little mosquito net to protect me! We began trapping them and Jo and her daughter would come and take them away. I wondered every time I came home what would be running around my house. Things that were left on the counter would be on the kitchen floor in the morning, and on New Year's morning I woke up to a big piece of rat poo right in the middle of my soft gray bathroom mat!

There is nothing honorable about rats. Yet I stayed…for 11 months. Why? Because my WHY was bigger than my fear of rats. Previous to this experience, I had never touched a hamster or held a guinea pig or even a rabbit. I screamed when there was a mouse in our apartment in Ecuador and jumped on the bed until my husband got rid of it. Yet now I lived with the rats. That's a mighty big why that got me through that massive fear.

How big is your why? It needs to be big, really big, for you to create the life you say you want to create. So get clear on your why, and then world, watch out! You're coming through. It's really that simple. And as you get clear on your why, watch all of the non-supporting beliefs show up so magnificently for you to see. "You're not good enough to have that. You're not important enough. Why do you deserve that? You can't afford that. You never stick with anything. You're not rich enough, young enough, or old enough." Watch them all come up and let them go at a DNA and cellular level. You can have what you want. You really can. Promise!

         Getting Off the Merry-Go-Round

Chapter Forty-Nine...

The little girl jumped into the deep end of the pool splashing me as I was doing my water aerobics. Her small head came bobbing up. She blinked her eyes, sputtered for a moment and climbed out as quick as a mouse to do it again. This time as she came up, she announced in a very clear voice, "My name is Olivia. I'm four years old."

Olivia was quite the character. In her little floral swimsuit, Olivia was everywhere at once. Before I had done ten more jumping jacks, Olivia jumped in again, bopped up and pulled a big wad of green gum out of her mouth, stretched in between her two hands and shoved it back in her mouth. "She could choke" was my first thought. My second thought was, "Where are the parents?" Mom and Dad, Grandma and Grandpa were all busy at the end of the pool socializing while their children played uproariously in the pool. No one was concerned or fretting. No one was even watching. Apparently no one except me was worried about Olivia's wad of gum choking her. Olivia had no fear of the water. She just knew that when she jumped in, she would come up.

I thought back to my own swimming lessons at six years of age. I was terrified. Repeating beginners level for the third time, I was with children much younger than me. I hated the water. I wasn't putting my face in it, and I most certainly wasn't going in over my head. Fear is for the most part learned. There are basic fears we all have, but Mom and Dad have a tremendous impact on how many fears we develop and how we respond to fear. We've all seen and heard parents who never stop nagging, "Don't do that, you'll fall, watch out, be careful, you're getting dirty, you're going to get hurt," and so on and so on. That poor child learns that whatever he or she does is dangerous. It's a heavy burden we carry.

It was truly delightful to see that Olivia hadn't been burdened with any of those beliefs when it came to the water.

Imagine running for a plane. You are about to leave with your small carry-on and head for the gate when the attendant says, "Sir, you have to take all of the passenger's luggage with you." You'd stop, defeated. What's the point? You'd never make it, so why bother trying? That's what it's like for us carrying all of these beliefs, fears and programs that aren't even ours.

Maybe Mom had a father who threw her in the pool and she remembers nearly drowning. She is now passing her fear on to her children every time she reminds them they can drown if they're not careful. After losing his father at the tender age of seven and experiencing his family's resulting struggles, my dad acquired a fear of not having enough materially. He remembered walking in the bitterly cold Winnipeg, Manitoba winters without shoes and developed an addiction to expensive shoes. The memory also fueled his insistence that I learn how to sew so I could clothe myself. I hated sewing but Dad was adamant. For every stitch I sewed, I picked out a dozen. Yet Dad was determined I learn to sew, despite the tears, the frustration and the obvious lack of joy. It was a skill I acquired, going on to take tailoring, but I have the Sacred Gift of Planning, not the Sacred Gift of Craftsmanship, so I would walk into a fabric store enthralled with the potential for the clothes, buy fabric, and never get the piece of clothing sewed.

Dad's fear was in every pattern and bag of fabric that lay forgotten like molding leftovers shoved to the back of the fridge. So on top of Dad's fear that I unknowingly inherited was my guilt over not finishing projects I started and being wasteful and a host of other negative emotions. I wasn't procrastinating, although on the surface it may have appeared that way. I simply had no passion and was being inspired by fear—a really lousy motivator.

As you create the life you really want, note what emotions you are using as your foundation because it is easy to have F – E – A – R as the four cornerstones.

Chapter Fifty...

Mom and Dad. They are two essential components to our life here on Earth, but oh my, what a mixed blessing most parents are. Part of being a parent is instilling in children thoughts, programs and beliefs that parents believe to be true. I remember my grandfather living with us after my grandmother passed away. An avid racist, he would watch the TV show "The Price is Right" and yell, "Those goddamn niggers!" every time a black person was chosen from the audience. I was twelve years old at the time and still vividly recall Grandpa's rage at someone with skin of a different color. Thankfully, I was simultaneously receiving very strong anti-racist training at the Kingdom Halls of the Jehovah's Witnesses, as we were a multi-national organization and acceptance of another person's color of skin was expected. If I hadn't had training to offset my Grandfather's outrageous bigotry, how would I feel today about people of a different race? Probably very differently.

In working with clients from all different backgrounds, I am at times stunned at how brutal, offensive and torturous parents can be with their children. The physical, emotional, mental and sexual abuse is often overwhelming. Parents definitely have an effect on their children, and it isn't always for the good. Cathy's dad was away at war when she was born and didn't return home until she was two years old. Her mother, excited by the return of her husband, wasn't expecting him to return an angry alcoholic. Little Cathy, so excited to have her new daddy home, wasn't prepared emotionally for the distant, violent and abusive father she received.

Decades later, Cathy is still trying to be "good enough," still tormented by her desire to do better, please more people, and appease everyone because, if even her own daddy didn't love her, why should anyone else? It has created a financial nightmare in Cathy's life because she gives away her work so easily in hopes that she will be loved. I am sure her dad went through a tremendous amount of trauma fighting a war, saw ugly things and had to do things that pained his very soul, but Cathy also reaped the effects of his life. Even now in her advanced years, Cathy is paying a high price for Dad's emotional state during her formative years.

Judy, on the other hand, is a different example of parental upbringing. She lives in my building here in Mazatlán.

Taught to play chess and surf at the formative age of four, Judy heard two words continuously as she was growing up: "You can." Judy learned from her parents that she could do anything she wanted. Given an allowance of 25 cents a week from the time she was five years old, Judy learned about financial independence early on as she put 15 cents of that in a savings account from day one.

Judy has never let anyone intimidate her as she entered male-dominated arenas for work and play. She became a mathematician by profession and an avid chess player and surfer.

In 1975 she met a challenge that would stop most people in their tracks. Her neck was broken in a horrible car accident, and Judy was told she would never walk again. Her response: "Get me a different doctor."

A year later, walking, but still in pain, she learned of a surfing competition in Mazatlán. She entered the competition as the only woman—and won.

Today Judy is about 70 years of age and has lived in Mexico since 1984. She lives a life that is full and busy. You'll find her playing board or card games around the pool with other residents, doing crossword or Sudoku, or teaching boogie boarding down at the beach.

I interviewed her one day in hopes of getting insight into her fascinating life. While speaking with Judy, you can feel her passion and intensity for women's rights, as fiery as the bright red lipstick she wears. There is nothing timid or pale about Judy. No subtle "pretty in pink" philosophy as she spoke out about female circumcision, the rape of women in the Congo in Africa and her views on religion. Everything you "aren't supposed to talk about," Judy had a mighty strong opinion about. I had known her up to that time as the woman who loved Yahtzee and crib, who always had a good book by the pool, who was going to teach me how to boogie board this summer once the ocean warmed up. I had no idea what strength and fire was in Judy, but once I got her started, I could just sit back and listen.

At the end of my interview with Judy, which had gone much longer than I had anticipated, she said to me, "That's all. You're done." I suspect Judy was just warming up.

Judy had been given a very great gift by her parents—the gift of confidence. She said to me, "my mother, who is still alive at 92, always saw me as the center of her universe." Judy learned early on to be the most important person in her own life. Judy learned from her parents how to see what she wanted, go for it, and not let anybody stop her. These are valuable lessons from parents that unfortunately haven't been passed on often enough.

So what do we do with what Mom and Dad have instilled in us? First of all, we recognize that they did their best. Even if they tortured you, abused you, or didn't love you the way you were hoping, they did the best they could with what they were working with at the time. My grandfather was kicked in the stomach by a horse and died when my father was just seven. Dad now had to step up to the plate and be "the man of the house." That's a tremendous responsibility for someone at that age, but I hear that phrase all the time from clients who were expected at tender ages to take on massive responsibility in times of crisis.

Do you think losing his dad at seven had an impact on my father? Absolutely.

My mother was an only child whose parents fought violently at times. When my mother playfully told her mom, "I'm too beautiful, don't look at me," when she was just a young girl, my grandmother grabbed her hair and cut off her beautiful long locks. My mother remembers having to prepare dinner alone for her parents when she was five and to clean up the blood after one of their fights. But my grandmother also ran a garage in Winnipeg with 30 mechanics in the early 1920s and was a brilliant entrepreneur. At a young age, Mom learned more about cars than most men would ever know, and she put in her days at the garage along with the men, including her own father.

Do you think those incidents made a difference in how my mother raised her children? You bet.

Your parents have similar stories. The tragedies may be different, but our parents went through a lot. They grew up in a time when personal development and workshops were unheard of and when expressing your emotions or even acknowledging them were considered unimportant luxuries. Emotions were shut down and locked in the back of the closet with the key thrown out. So the first step is to acknowledge that your parents did the best they could under the circumstances, and although it may look pretty pathetic for their best, trust that it was, and forgive. Whether they are still alive or dead, the only person you are hurting by holding on to the pain your parents caused you is you. So let it go and let's move on, shall we?

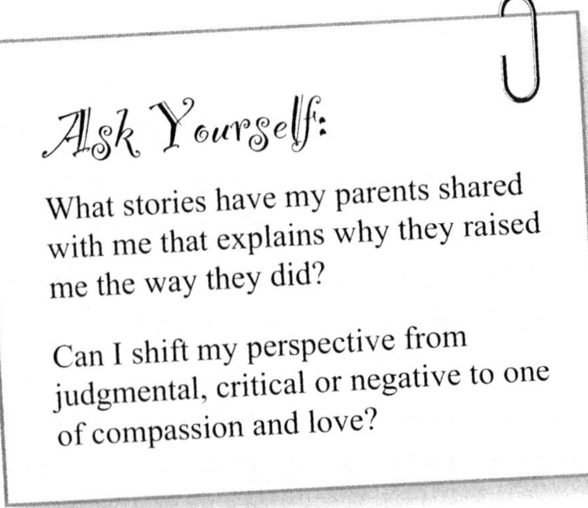

Chapter Fifty-One...

Part of letting go of our parent's effect is to realize where you are punishing yourself because of Mom and Dad. What do I mean by that? Let me introduce you to Julie.

Julie's parents had worked hard for their wealth and had achieved a very comfortable lifestyle. Julie, however, had never been acknowledged for her efforts. Her brother had stolen the show. "Just the girl" in the family, nothing Julie did was ever enough. It was never recognized and never valued. Julie grew up fighting for her parent's love.

Upon their death, Julie received an inheritance of more than a quarter of a million dollars. Within a short period of time, the money was gone and Julie was bankrupt. What happened? In going back over the events emotions, programs and beliefs Julie was operating from, it soon became apparent that Julie had punished her parents by "pissing away" their money, to use her words. Her parents, who had worked so hard for this money, had established a solid reputation in the community and were respected for their wealth and for being "good people," had left behind a daughter who in that very same community created a financial mess for herself. It caused shame and embarrassment in her own life, but also a big black stain on her parent's grave. Her parent's hard-earned money now gone forever, Julie had punished her parents for their lack of love and recognition of her AND created a financial disaster for herself.

Are you still punishing your parents for something they didn't give you—attention, recognition, love, respect—by sabotaging an area of your life? Look at where your life isn't working like you want it to and see if this could be an issue for you.

I was a slob because of this very situation. My chaotic, disorganized, untidy lifestyle was my way of getting back at my parents for their incredible control. Having everything from the length of my skirt to what movies, books and friends I could enjoy to what level of education I might pursue controlled by my parents, my slovenliness was a blatant way to say to Mom and Dad, "You are not telling me what to do."

Once I healed that issue, I literally went from being one of the three little pigs to maintaining a sense of order and organization that still amazes me. Imagine having clothes hung up, bed made, dishes washed, files filed, keys up on the key chain and shoes put away together—all novel concepts for me in the last few years. When I healed this in me, Mom was living her last year confined to a nursing home, and Dad hadn't talked to me in years and certainly wasn't coming to visit. The daily mess I created in my life was hurting one person and one person only—me. Mom and Dad would never see it or suffer because of it. So if you identify in some way that you are punishing Mom and Dad for your upbringing, it really is time to let it go. They aren't hurting because of it—only you are.

Ask Yourself:

- In what areas of my life today am I punishing Mom and Dad for my upbringing?

- What emotions does it trigger in me?

To Do...

Release them at a DNA and cellular level. For help with this, collect your bonus gift at www.anamazinglifenow.com Password is Brenda.

Chapter Fifty-Two...

Families can be challenging. There is a saying that we choose our friends but not our families. That saying implies there is often friction between family members, and that is probably true. Especially as we are trying to move ahead in our life and create an amazing life, we may be surprised at how unsupportive family members can be. What we think is fabulous, they turn their noses up at. What excites us, they think is horrible. What motivates us, depresses them. This is where two core beliefs—that it doesn't matter what anybody thinks about you and that you are the most important person in your life— really need to come to the fore.

My father, still a devout Jehovah's Witness, doesn't approve of my lifestyle, my ministry or just about anything else he knows about me—and he doesn't know the half of what I do! He talks to me once in a while, but the tenor and tone of these calls is hard to deny: he phones to see if I am unhappy yet, if I am ready to come back to the fold of the religion he loves, or if I am marrying the man I sleep with. In other words, it's not my most favorite conversation of the year, needless to say. But I have learned to have those conversations with no fear, doubt or guilt because I am convinced my life works for me and that's all that matters.

I appreciate where Dad is coming from. It's a perspective I once shared, one based in fear and guilt. Dad sometimes seems to forget that he left two previous religions before he became a Jehovah's Witness, that he has had his share of infidelity, and that he isn't exactly a poster child for JOY. So I love him for where he's at, and at 85 years of age, realize the days with my dad are numbered. A sister and brother of mine also have nothing to do with me, because of differences in opinion on their part. I'd talk to the whole lot of them—they don't bother me one bit, but I respect that I simply may not be their cup of tea. It makes life really easy as I travel the world, have incredible freedom and make choices. Those are all compensations for a family that doesn't really like me. I have no obligations to them, which I see as a blessing because there is no point seeing it any other way.

My one sister who is open to my way of living keeps in touch with me, and we have a great time catching up with each other regularly. I could worry and feel guilty over the family relationships, but as I am the most important person in my life, my only question is, "Does it work for me?" And it honestly does, because I honor and respect their opinions and if they can't do the same for me, it's not my problem. It's theirs, 100 percent of it.

In her book *Feel the Fear and Do It Anyway*, Susan Jeffers talks about a no-lose approach to life, a concept I have really grasped and modeled. You may want to embrace it also. Simply stated, Dr. Jeffers says to look at everything from a no-lose perspective. If my family were close and huggy like some, then there would be awesome family get-togethers, lots of fun, and family vacations. There would be a camaraderie that one can only enjoy with family. Awesome benefits, and I am sure there are more. On the other hand, the distance that I have in my family provides me with freedom, no responsibilities, and the ability to choose friends who are amazing and like-minded.

You can do the same with every aspect of your life. Stay home and there are advantages. Travel the world and there are benefits. Have a family and there are perks. Stay childless and there are bonuses. Get the point? I really like this model for life because it keeps me constantly focused on what a great life I have no matter what is happening. I could miss the family vacations but they aren't going to happen so why put energy into such a futile thought process. People whine and complain about stuff they can't ever change—a really big waste of time. Watch where you are moaning and groaning and then find a no-lose approach to every situation. No exceptions…none. It's quite remarkable how much happier you will be.

     Getting Off the Merry-Go-Round

Chapter Fifty-Three...

It's easy to blame everything else. It's the government, the weather, the lousy boss, the dishonest employee, the crooked accountant, the lazy lawyer, the cheating partner, the bad economy. Find someone to blame quick! It can't possibly be my fault, and as I have shown, it's really easy to blame parents.

Wayne Dyer tells the story of one of his younger daughters being quite indignant about his parenting skills. She was appalled that he actually taught people how to be good parents, as she felt he was so woefully inadequate as one. One day Wayne stopped her dead in her tracks when he said that she should stop blaming him and Mom and take responsibility. She looked at him with her hands on her hips and asked, "Why should I take responsibility for your parenting?"

Wayne replied, "Because before you came to Earth, you chose Mom and me to be your parents."

She was stunned. "I chose you and Mom to be my parents?" He assured her that before she came to Earth this time, she had made her choice of parents and he and his wife had been completely her choice. She looked at him incredulously and said, "Well I must have been in an awfully big hurry!"

I never fail to chuckle at that story because I do believe that we chose our parents. Some of us essentially chose storks for parents. You know the story some parents told their children in lieu of teaching them about sex. A stork brought you to Mom and Dad. Well, I do believe many parents are simply the vehicles through which our souls chose to come to this Earth. Our souls didn't want a tremendous amount of nurturing or direction. We needed a home so we could get our feet wet and then go out and do the work we were here to do.

I am amazed at how many clients I work with spent some time away from parents, either given up for adoption, in foster care, or shipped out while the parent went through a crisis. My mother gave me over to the care of an older couple for the first six months of my life, while she regained her health. It's very common—much more so than I would have thought. Were our parents simply storks in the broadest sense of the term? Perhaps. I am truly grateful for much of the training I received in the family I chose, as it has prepared me well for my Assignment here on Earth. It wasn't an easy choice, but I have reconciled that I made the choice and made peace with the decision.

Can you do the same? Accepting the fact that you chose Mom and Dad to be your earthly parents, your brothers and sisters to be part of your life, and all the accoutrements that came with that choice, makes life a whole lot easier. Start looking at the good that came out of the situation. Begin finding the benefits that the hardships caused, the ability they gave you to handle adversity, challenge or problems, and appreciate that you wouldn't be who you are today if things had been different. I'd never have the ability to deal with people of all beliefs, customs and backgrounds if I hadn't grown up being trained in a door-to-door ministry where you had no idea who was behind each and every door. I would never be able to confidently speak in front of thousands if I hadn't been trained in public speaking from the age of eight. And I would certainly never have the focus and discipline to write a book in less than two months for the second time if I hadn't been well-trained to adhere to a strict schedule.

You can do the same. Start appreciating what Mom and Dad gave you, even if the beatings taught you discipline, even if the lack of love taught you the importance of love, even if the abuse taught you compassion for others—those are all valuable lessons, don't you think?

Blame is a really big crutch. You chose Mom and Dad. You started creating your life BEFORE you even got here to Earth, and it hasn't changed since. You created it, you are creating it moment by moment, and you will continue to create it until the moment you die. In the very moment that your breath, your Spirit returns to the Universe, you will create either an environment of peace, joy and love or one of fear, resentment and anger. It's a very powerful place to understand that once you stop complaining about all the things you can't change such as your parents, the weather, the economy or the world, you really move into a magnificent place. You can only change yourself and that's powerful.

So what changes are you making?

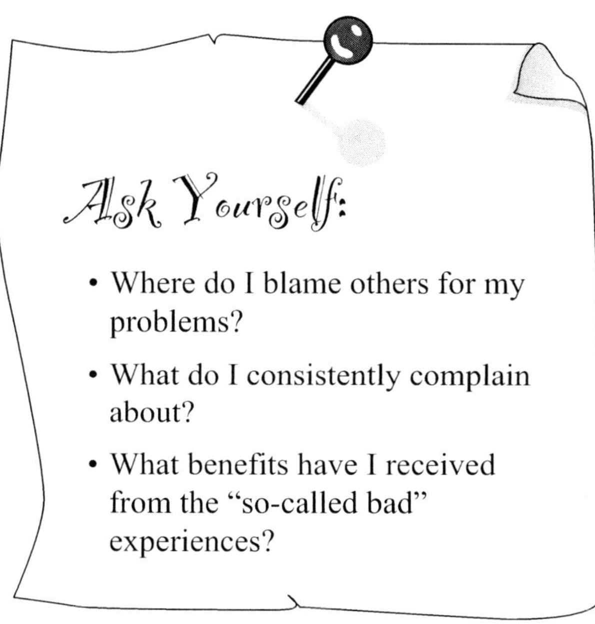

Chapter Fifty-Four...

You may be feeling a bit overwhelmed as you begin to appreciate how complex you are. I remember at times feeling like I was Alice, falling down a deep, dark hole. I still hadn't touched bottom. Would I ever?

The equilibrium and the sanity met up somewhere along the line, and I just knew that something big had shifted. The peace that I had known was possible was staying around longer, not just dropping in for a cup of tea. I had invited it to spend the night, and when it finally did, it didn't leave first thing in the morning but stayed for awhile, like a new lover. But then, by the time I got out of the shower, it would be gone. I'd wonder what I had done or said to chase it away. I'd pray it would come back and favor me again.

Days, weeks, even months later, I would wake up and feel the peace and thank God that I was in his grace just one more day. Like any new lovers, it was a tentative relationship. Would he be okay with my cellulite? Would he think my breasts were too small? Could I really please him, or would he be comparing me with his last girlfriend? It felt exactly that unsure and unfamiliar living in that place of peace. And yet the peace stayed longer. Days melted into nights and nights into days with the comfortableness of an old married couple. Anxiety turned to anticipation and expectation morphed into reality. It was a beautiful courtship.

Court peace as you would a lover. How do you do that? Just as you pay extra attention to your personal grooming when newly dating, pay extra attention to your emotions while courting peace. Are you complaining, bitching and grumbling about the weather, the traffic, the kids, the job, the boss, the finances and the government? Notice that. New lovers don't want to know you're overdrawn at the bank, your kid is on drugs and you may be downsized next month. They want you to talk to them about niceties, prettiness and romance. They want to enjoy the sunset, savor the food, and play with sex. Romance peace in your life by focusing on the beauty around you and the abundance you enjoy.

And lighten up! Have some fun and let go of the stress, and peace will become a more welcome bedfellow. Invite it to stay daily with words such as "May this day be one of peace for me and for everyone I meet," or "Thank you for allowing me to be in your grace today, God." Peace is a natural quality of Spirit. Your five CEOs love to be in a place of peace—they just haven't known it for a long, long time. Love peace, pray for peace, and live in peace. By doing so, you spread a wonderful vibration of peace.

What a gift to the world!

Chapter Fifty-Five...

Does it serve? No, this isn't a tennis match—although life may often feel like it is one and you are the ball, being smacked over the net, back and forth, back and forth. That is the question to ask yourself daily —does it serve? In other words, is this working? Do I like the results?

Now you can't actually ask that question until you are very clear on what you are wishing to attain. Does it serve what? Your vision, your dreams, your plans—what you want to do, who you want to be, what you want to have. Yes, you must get some clarity on those questions BEFORE there is any point asking, "Does it serve?" Once you know the direction you are headed, you can know whether or not an action, a decision, a career choice, a financial plan, or anything else in your life is actually bringing you closer or further away from where you are headed. No point getting on a plane to go to Dallas when you want to head to Singapore.

"But, but, but…I have no choice." I've heard some incredibly evolved people complain about a situation with the words, "I have no choice." Ah, but you do. You ALWAYS have choice. So you can ask about situations, events, people and decisions in your life: Does it serve? Do I like the results I am getting? If not, change the action that is creating the results. If you don't like being broke because that puts you in a place of fear and guilt, then change your actions. Spend too much? Spend less. Earn too little? Earn more. If you don't like where you live, move. If hanging out with a group of people who don't have your values, goals and aspirations is no longer working for you, then don't keep going out with them on Saturday night. Change friends. If you are sick, get healthy. If you are fat, lose weight. You see, you have choice, but more importantly, you are powerful.

You are so incredibly powerful, in fact, you can do anything you want. The Spirit that is operating in you is the same Spirit that created the sun, moon and stars. It is the same Spirit that moves the tides. Have you ever moved a waterbed mattress? If it even has a few cups of water left in it, you will be amazed at how heavy it is. Yet every day, Spirit moves oceans that cover more than half of this globe's surface. Don't you think such a Spirit can manage your life? Wouldn't you agree that you are probably less complex than creating the entire Milky Way Galaxy? The answer to that question may admittedly depend on the time of the month for you or your bank balance at this moment—but seriously, our lives, as complex as they are, are truly simple when compared to the big issues that Spirit deals with on a daily basis. Remember that. YOU ARE POWERFUL.

So back to the question: Does it serve? Start eliminating what isn't working, including beliefs, people, ideas, programs, and habits, then start asking Spirit to invite in peace, love, joy, prosperity, abundance, happiness, fun, play, great relationships, amazing friends, fabulous sex and any other wonderful thing you wish to see present in your life. With the simple question "Does it serve?" your life can change dramatically.

To Do:

Pick one area in your life you're not happy with and change ONE thing today.

Example: *No money.*

Find one bill that could be reduced or eliminated.

Chapter Fifty-Six...

Sometimes we can be so frickin' stubborn. We need to be right. And much like the four-year-old throwing the temper tantrum in the middle of the kitchen floor, we will insist on our own way, even when we know full well that it is not in our highest and best interest.

I know I am probably not talking about you personally in this chapter, but perhaps you can relate to someone you know who always needs to be right. If the weather is bad, they were right. You shouldn't have gone. If the weather is good, they were right. You should have done something different. If the relationship works out, they were right.

Why do we need to be right? This is one explanation: At some point in time, probably in early childhood, you used one of your Sacred Gifts. Perhaps it was the Gift of Wisdom or the Gift of Organization or the ability to connect with the other side. You weren't even aware of it. It just happened and out of your mouth, popped words of wisdom, clearly pointing out the answer or solution to a problem. Or you took charge and got something done because the big picture was so obvious to you. Perhaps as is the case for many children gifted with the ability to communicate with the supernatural, you talked about the angels, or fairies or the dead Grandma that you had just had a conversation with.

Parents, in their own place of insecurity, in their own place of being in "safe mode" and seeing the world as dangerous, coupled with their past lives, genetic coding and beliefs, shut you down. Angered because you knew in your soul that you were right, you now go on a rampage that you need to be right. You need to be listened to. You need to be valued. You must be respected. Or else, you're angry! I remember an incident when I was about seven years old. My six-month-old nephew was sitting in his high chair at the cabin the family had rented for the week. Someone put hot soup on his highchair tray to feed him and he stuck his hand straight into it and burned himself. After all the screaming, wailing and hysteria passed, I made what seemed like an obvious comment: "You shouldn't have put the hot soup on his tray."

That night as my father passed me in the hallway as I was headed to bed, I got smacked across the head and told that I had no business saying what I did. For years, I remembered that incident with anger, hatred and frustration that my dad hadn't appreciated my comment. It stuck with me like a file with a large red flag that said, "When you voice your wisdom, you get into trouble."

As I grew up in a male-dominated religion, other incidents throughout my lifetime reaffirmed that when I spoke up, deep trouble followed. It seriously affected my respect for men and put my own intelligence in question, which brings up those old, self-defeating questions: *Am I good enough? Do I really know what I am talking about? Will anybody think I'm an expert?* It confirmed for me that I shouldn't use my voice, even when I knew I was right.

Another reason we need to be right is that it is a survival technique. If you're right, you get to live. If you're right, you just might survive. All of us have had some past lives that were challenging, when we suffered unjustly, when we were misunderstood. The file is, "If I am wrong, I die."

I have had many clients who lived in terror of making a mistake, being wrong or being seen as different. Why? Because the memories were very strong of lifetimes where they were tortured or abused. At one workshop, I referred to someone being afraid of their gift of healing because of past life experiences, such as having their tongue cut out. A woman later told me that the moment I said that, she experienced a jolt in the very core of her being.

I had never said that before to anyone, particularly not in a group of business people and employees, but it came out of my mouth that day, obviously just for her. She realized there was a deep fear inside of her around her present-day gift of healing.

Survival is always paramount. Once you understand that it may not even be a present-day belief that you need to be right, but is an old file, you can let it go, heal it, and move into a greater place of peace.

Ask Yourself:

- Do I need to be right?

- Why do I get angry, upset, afraid or feel out of control when I am wrong?

- Do I believe I am "bad" if I am wrong?

Chapter Fifty-Seven...

Will it be Rome this week, or India? The Vatican—or the Taj Mahal? Let me think about that. So you've created the life of your dreams. You're doing the work you love. You've been to far-flung places like Machu Picchu and Stonehenge. You've done the African safari. You've still got Egypt on the calendar for the year and it's not even summer. However, as much as you feel fabulous about what you have done, where you have gone, what you have accomplished, there is something inside of you that just doesn't feel right.

This is the life of one of my clients. She really is the globetrotter of the century. She has a great business, incredible kids, wonderful health, fabulous friends—yet deep inside, she feels guilty. A fifty-something modern woman, my client has what most women just decades ago could never have imagined enjoying. Yet something is wrong.

As we worked through this feeling, a few critical things came up. Her dad had worked very hard to build a family inheritance. He did such a magnificent job that now, 35 years later, with both parents gone, she is enjoying the benefits of Dad's hard work and the sacrifices he made over half a century ago. While she is doing her best to learn about investments and money management, there is a part of her that feels like she is disrespecting her Dad's money and certainly not honoring what he gave his life to achieve. The trips, the fun, the art classes on Friday all come with a high price tag—guilt over spending Dad's money, worry that she'll spend all the money and have nothing for old age (the bag lady syndrome), and fear that she won't fit in with her friends anymore, as no one else in her crowd can do what she is doing.

Issues around money are deep. Fear of losing it, fear of having it, fear of having more than anyone else we know, fear of being seen as a "rich bitch," lazy, spoilt, a "kept" woman, and a multitude of other beliefs hold people in their economic position in life. In working with another client, a very professional career woman, similar beliefs showed up with a twist. She was ready to move to the next level of her life, but a fear of "can I really move out of my circle and into the next" and "do I really deserve to leave behind the Tribe and move into another arena" were her predominant thoughts. If you have only ever eaten at McDonald's, you would think the food was fine. Now go to a five-star restaurant for dinner and compare it with McDonald's. You may never be satisfied again eating at McDonald's.

That brings up two major fears around money. One: If I really do move up the ladder, then I will not be satisfied with what I have now. Which in turn brings a second major fear: all sorts of pressure as you begin to realize that your clothes don't suit, your furnishings aren't posh enough, you may not live in the right neighborhood, your manners may not match the upper-class—in short, your whole lifestyle is out of sync with a higher standard of living.

There is a Tribal Mentality belief that if you earn more money, you have to show it and look the part. There are exceptions, of course— Sam Walton drove around in his old Ford truck, despite being an extremely wealthy man. But most people still believe at a cellular and Subconscious Mind level that their life will change dramatically if they earn more money, and subsequently they simply won't fit in. There's a dress code and a way of being that is expected for the five-star restaurant. Old jeans and running shoes with holes in them simply don't cut it. Now you have to learn which fork to use and which glass on the side of the plate is yours. There is a different level of conversation. You need to know your wine list, rather than just buying the cheapest beer at the store. There's a vocabulary that is required.

As my client faced those fears of being "good enough" for a whole different level of financial success, she also realized that she really, really, *really* wanted to be there. She liked the five-star restaurants. She liked the nice clothes. She liked earning a very nice six-figure income and all the perks that go along with that. There will always be

     Getting Off the Merry-Go-Round

a clientele for McDonald's and for the five-star restaurant. There will always be people traveling in coach while others jet-set across the globe in a private jet.

What you need to get really honest about is the million dollar question: What do I really, really, *really* want? You see, people THINK they want to be millionaires, but then as they earn more money, they realize that a certain expectation comes with more wealth and you will change. Some of my clients have phoned me angrily after a few sessions. Why? Because now that we have raised their level of self-esteem, they are no longer happy being broke, living in a mess, or being overweight. They've been all those things up until now, and although those things may have bothered them, they weren't in their face. Now they are. Now they have to come to terms with many deeper and surrounding issues in their lives. Change is happening, and it's uncomfortable.

Money is a complex issue as my two clients discovered. We hold a lot of energy around money which is also fascinatingly unnecessary. Why do I say that? Because money is actually very simple, as you'll learn in the next chapter.

To Do:

Either have a conversation with a friend or partner about money OR write a paragraph or more about how you really feel about money.

Chapter Fifty-Eight...

Air, water, and food are all staples much of the human race takes for granted. All are forms of energy. Without getting into a philosophical or political discussion on the sustainability of any of these components moving into the 21st century, let's just agree that we all need air, water and food and that we get them daily.

Can money be in the same category? For sure! Air, water, food, and money. Money, water, food and air. Same energy, different forms. Just as you don't get up in the morning and immediately think, "I sure hope there's going to be enough air today," why would you get up in the morning and think, "I sure hope there's going to be enough money to pay the bills today"? I doubt you drive to your local grocery store and think, "I hope there's food on the shelf at the supermarket. I hope it's not closed or empty." Why then do you worry that when you open your bank account, it will be empty? Unless you have lived in a developing country like I have, where water didn't necessarily come out of my taps every day, you turn on your taps for a shower in the morning and expect water. You don't even give it a second thought. On goes the water and you jump in.

So why do you worry so much about the money flow in your life?

We make a BIG deal about money. An inordinate amount of energy and thought is put into money. Making it, keeping it, safeguarding it, losing it, earning it, protecting it, growing it, investing it, spending it, saving it—the list goes on and on and on. It's insane. We'd never go to a "How to get enough air in your life" workshop, would we?

I hope you're laughing at how the Tribe makes this whole area of money a massive merry-go-round that is ridiculous. Why do we spend so much energy on something as simple as money? You see, the more you worry over it and talk about it, the more it gets completely blown out of proportion in your Subconscious Mind. It's like you're telling the Subconscious Mind, "This is a hard thing to get, to keep and to have."

I suggest strongly that you relax about money. View it like air, water and food and expect it to be there. I EXPECT when I open my fridge there will be food if I have done my grocery shopping for the week. I EXPECT there to be water for my shower if I have paid my water bill for the month. I EXPECT when I open my bank account that there will be money if I have done my work for the week. Pretty simple formula. I use less air than exists. I use less water than is available. I eat less food than I can buy. I spend less money than I earn. No big deal. RELAX about money.

Now I know that goes completely contrary to what everyone is telling you. There are enough money workshops to last you a lifetime. There are enough money newsletters to read for an entire year. There is enough advice out there about money to make you dizzy. Yet, going back to my touchstone for everything: What are the results? Not particularly impressive for all the information out there on money. Two-thirds of the world lives either in poverty or so close to it that it's frightening. You don't need to be a rocket scientist to figure out that the world view on money is not working.

Start with two simple philosophies. First: Money is another energy, just like air, water and food. Start thinking of it as automatic, expected and as simple as that. Air, water, food, money. If you raised a child isolated from all of the Tribal Mentalities around money and taught the child that money was just like air, food, and water, that child would not have all the emotional charge around money that we do.

It truly is a Tribal Mentality belief that money is hard to come by. Why can I say that? Trillions of dollars passed hands today. How many of those dollars passed through your hands? You see, money circulates. Every day. The only question is how much circulated through your life. If you are standing in the river of money and you're there with a teaspoon, you get a teaspoon of money. If you're there with a bucket, you get a bucket of money. If you're there with a dump truck, you'll get a dump truck of money. If you don't even bother going to the river of money, you'll get—you guessed it—nothing.

If you didn't breathe, would you get air? If you didn't turn on the water tap, would you get water? If you didn't open the refrigerator, would you get food? So why do you have another view around money? It's exactly the same principle. Get in the river of money and get your share. It's happening—with or without you.

Second philosophy: Start focusing on how much you earn rather than on how much you spend. Remember, I was once almost bankrupt. So how did I change my poverty mentality to one of abundance? One of the most effective exercises I did was to start keeping track of my income rather than my expenses. Just like I expect food, water and air every day in my life, I expected money every day in my life. I started keeping track of where money was coming into my life. It was quite remarkable. I went from money coming into my life about six days a month to twenty-eight days a month. Do you think that had an effect on my income? You bet! Every night before I went to bed, I wrote down where money came from and how much. Maybe I got paid out on an affiliate program that day. Perhaps the government sent me a check. A client paid me. I sold a book. I found money. I got paid interest on a bank account. I made it into a really fun game and every day would wait with eager expectation and anticipation to see where money was going to come from today. To this day, I love depositing money and watching my bank account grow. I barely think about my expenses except that I consistently spend less than I earn.

Interestingly, I have now programmed my subconscious that I earn more than I spend. It's a pretty simple program to create wealth. I wasn't even aware of how ingrained this now was in my team until the first six weeks here in Mexico. I wasn't working, yet my spending was continuing as I rented a condo and still hadn't sold my car, so I had lease payments and insurance along with the normal expenses of day-to-day living.

I noticed how uncomfortable I was after the two-week holiday with Greg was over. I was now on my own. I didn't realize that the programming was very much in place, thanks to all the work I had done, that I am comfortable ONLY when I earn more than I spend. I'm happy to spend less, but I must earn more. I LIKE that program, and it now happens so automatically that the bank account just grows without any stress. You gotta love that!

One thing that I have noticed consistently with clients is that they are pretty apathetic or angry about money. Either they are pissed off because there's not enough, angry at the scrimping that is going on in their life OR they couldn't care less at some level. They are hardly excited about this beautiful energy we call money.

In working with clients, I will often ask them what they are going to do with the extra money they receive. They can't tell me. All they see is debt. Let me tell you, your team does not get excited about debt. Even when they do tell me what they would do, there is an air of resignation that it will never happen, so they are cautious in their excitement meter. Get rid of that nonsense! Get excited about money, what you want to do, what you need the money for, and the good things you want to do for yourself and for your family. Make a big deal out of your plans for the money. Get into the emotions. With one client, we starting envisioning together what it would be like for her children to travel the world, help other kids in less privileged countries, for her to have a housecleaner and to get back to singing lessons.

By the time, we finished, she was excited. Without a reason and an awareness of the EMOTIONS involved with that reason, there is nothing to juice your team. Flatline life and your team is dead, just like a heart monitor looking for a pulse that is nonexistent. Are you dead? I don't think so, but you may be acting like you are! Get into life, emotionally, physically, mentally, spiritually AND financially and you will be amazed at the results.

Do you see how simple money is? You can make it into a big deal, hard to come by, and a host of other nonsensical beliefs, but that will only keep money at arm's length. Money is just energy. It's just a thing. It is only what you decide it is. I suggest you make it as desirable as a breath of crisp mountain air at sunrise, as delectable as a five-star restaurant meal, as relaxing as a hot bath after a long day.

What do you want money to be in your life? The more positive emotions you attach to money, just like everything else in life, the more amazing your life will be. Back to choice. Choice about how you view it, how much you want of it and how much you keep of it. Isn't it exciting? The power is all yours. But by now, I bet you already knew that.

Chapter Fifty-Nine...

I can hear you now: *If it's really that simple, why don't I have any money, Jan?*

Great question! As I moved out of the financial mess I was in, that is a question I never stopped asking. As simple as I now understand money to be, I also realized that it was critically important. When you don't have enough, you really get that point loud and clear. Putting $5 worth of gas into your car at a time, not paying bills on time, and having medical issues with no money to deal with them are all scary realities when there's not enough money. It's also cripples your self-esteem and deflates your dreams, visions and goals when there is no money. It's humiliating and humbling. So please know that if you are currently in this situation, I've been there and understand.

Let's just move you past that, shall we?

One night while laying in bed talking to God, I asked two questions that changed a lot of things for me. The first question was: Does the Universe think I'm wealthy? The answer was YES. Next question was: Do I think I'm wealthy? The answer was YES.

I jumped out of bed with another one of my H.S. moments and got to work on myself. Of course, the Universe would think I was wealthy. I had a fridge full of food, including a freezer full of enough soup to feed half my community! I had a car in the garage with a tank full of gas. I had money in the bank and a closet full of clothes. I could go to the shopping mall and buy a plethora of material products—practically anything I wanted. I had a home with water and electricity 24/7. Compared to the majority of people in the world, I was wealthy. At some level, I wasn't fully appreciating my wealth and that needed to change. Big reminder on the importance of gratitude for what I already had.

Secondly, my definition of wealthy obviously wasn't clear. I needed to change that file. If you can remember one simple rule: Your results in life are ALWAYS, ALWAYS, ALWAYS a product of your thoughts and emotions. There are NO exceptions. You may not like that rule because you don't like your results, but it is the best rule in the Universe because it puts all of the choice, responsibility and power back in your hands. You may not like it because you want God to bless you, a man to provide for you, and the government to take care of you, but hopefully you are working at clearing some of those beliefs from you at a DNA and cellular level because they are disempowering to you. Get rid of your hang-ups around choice, responsibility and power while you're at it.

Thoughts + Emotions = Results.

What about the action part of the equation? We'll talk about that in a moment. So I simply needed to get clear on my definition of wealth and have a chat with the Universe that with much greater wealth, I could become a much greater conduit for good on this planet. With that end in mind, I asked to be trained, pruned and prepared for much greater wealth. I asked to be a steward of God's wealth here on Earth. Today, I am abundant, prosperous and moving very nicely toward my expanded definition of wealth and becoming a steward of God's wealth here on earth. It's been a journey, believe me.

Chapter Sixty...

What about the action?

You do need to take action, but action in my opinion should happen automatically. It comes back to my philosophy that life needs to be easy. So I could put in the equation Thoughts + Emotions + Action = Results and that would be absolutely correct. However, the action part, in my mind, should happen without my having to force myself, plan every detail, and stress about it. When I cleared the beliefs, programs and emotions around being a slob, the actions of hanging up my clothes, making my bed, putting away after myself, hanging the keys on the key chain, washing the dishes, filing the papers, and folding the laundry happened without an effort on my part. I wanted to do life differently, and I did. The synapses were now connected differently. New dendrites had been formed. Files were changed. I didn't consciously think about any of it. I work, believe me. I am busy. I get lots accomplished, but I don't stress about what may happen, should happen or will happen tomorrow, next week, next month or next year.

Staying in the present is really a gift. I tell God all the time, "Don't tell me all the good things that are coming. Surprise me!" And so I wait and watch like a kid at the candy store, knowing there are so many options and opportunities. I am delighted there is so much to look forward to while I completely enjoy the present.

I remember finishing up the year 2004 and thinking that if on January 1st of that year, you would have told me I was going to spend eight weeks volunteering in South Africa and would now own a pole dancing company, I would have asked you what you were smoking. What a delightful and unexpected surprise!

If on January 1st, 2007, I had heard that on December 31st, I would be madly in love with the most amazing man on the planet and moving to Mexico—well, perhaps I wouldn't have been too surprised, but those two things certainly weren't written in any business plan. They were, however, most definitely written in my heart. My team knew my desires, goals, visions and hopes. I had done my work, and now I let them do theirs.

My part was to do some journaling about relationships and to heal my issues around men. I knew there was someone very special coming. I had felt it in my heart for some months, but Greg exceeded my wildest expectations. I knew I wanted to leave Vancouver at some time. I knew I wanted to live in the sunshine. I knew I wanted to leave behind a more hectic way of life. I did not expect it to happen so quickly—but how perfect! So the action happened of its own volition. The ground had been plowed, the seeds had been sown, and then I let it happen naturally. All of you gardeners know that once you plant a seed, you can't be digging it up, examining it, and wondering why it hasn't sprouted yet. You have to let nature do its magic. The seed will grow IF you have done your work.

Do your work and let the rest happen. Relax. It's all a game. Enjoy it. Trust and have fun. It's much easier that way.

Just Note:

Where in my life do I feel the most stress?

Are emotions of impatience, lack of trust, feeling of not being in control contributing to the stress?

Let them go at a DNA and cellular level. Check www.anamazinglifenow.com to see what current resources I am offering to support you on your journey.

Chapter Sixty-One...

et's continue to dissect the subject of money as I know it's a major issue for most people.

Many of the beliefs we have around money come from parents. My parents had money for most of my years growing up, but I still found myself near bankruptcy. What happened? As I was raised in a religion where the world was always coming to an end, saving money wasn't important. There were no plans for the future because in paradise, where I was headed, we didn't need money. We needed faith—and that I had in abundant supply. My mother used to actually say to me, "Don't paint the stateroom Jan. You're on the Titanic." In other words, the world is going to hell in a hand basket, so don't worry about money—it doesn't matter. And so I didn't. I made some good money over the years working, usually part-time, so I could spend time in the ministry.

But when my husband and I left for Ecuador, he had quit a very good job with Canada Safeway. He had a nice retirement savings plan that we managed to get paid out, and off we went to serve as missionaries. Nobody even thought to tell us about living off the principal, even though interest rates in 1991 were 12% per annum, so it would have been easy enough for us to do that. We spent the money because we truly never expected to come back.

Then, after I left the Jehovah's Witnesses and started making a really good income, Stephen left. A need to rescue someone came up immediately, along with the need to be wanted, loved, and needed. So I found a partner who was almost bankrupt. Funding both of us in business ventures proved to be near fatal. There was a definite program that having money wasn't spiritual and entering into a really unhealthy relationship because of my issues around abandonment contributed to the financial fiasco.

I had watched my parents argue over money and learned that money divides a couple. I saw that my mother having "her own money" gave her some power over my father. She used it like a weapon to stake her independence and freedom. I watched my father never stay and pay off a house as we moved countless times into bigger and better homes. My parents could be very generous. I saw my family's wealth used to help others who were less fortunate, along with money being a real source of arrogant pride for my father who had been extremely poor as an immigrant child. It sent very mixed messages to my subconscious as to whether money was good or bad, wicked or evil, desirable or something to be shunned.

My family provides a good example of the distorted messages our parents received from their parents, who lived through wars and depressions. Money is seen as a "necessary evil." You need it, but you can't trust it, depend on it or love it, because it can turn on you at any time. Money is worse than a fickle lover. So the love/hate relationship is fostered, and all of these emotions are filed away as battles are fought, struggles are endured, and relationships are based on this little thing called money.

But that's not all.

Ask Yourself:

What beliefs around money did I get from Mom and Dad?

What negative or disempowering beliefs stand out?

Are those beliefs still affecting my finances today?

     Getting Off the Merry-Go-Round

Chapter Sixty-Two...

Genetic coding also plays a role in our views on money. Some of the European genetic coding that I have worked with has a more light-hearted approach to life. The Italians and the French, for example, know how to have fun, enjoy life and take life easy. On the other hand, the Polish, Ukrainian, Russian and many of the other European countries have a very strong work ethic drilled into them at a DNA and cellular level. You need to work hard, and there's an expectation of poverty and challenges. They don't really seem to believe, in their very core, that they will ever succeed financially.

Look at your own genetic coding and see what views around money your parents and grandparents (and so on) were raised in. It can definitely explain many reasons that you have issues around money. My background on my dad's side is Russian Mennonite with some gypsy and Dutch mixed in. The genetic coding I picked up is I didn't deserve to have money. I wasn't good enough as a woman to have money. Money was hard to come by, difficult to keep and unnecessary. Yet, both the Russian and the Dutch genetic coding affirmed I was supposed to work hard, the gypsy made me also want to be on the move, and there was definitely a "fun, free-spirited, eccentric, don't fit into the Tribe" coding there which helped balance the seriousness of the rest.

But for many people, genetic coding is why money slips through their fingers, they can't keep it, they are embarrassed by any amount of it or they see it as a burden. Too much work, too much responsibility, too much to think about can be part of your genetic coding, or the belief that money is only for the aristocratic, the elite, the powerful or for an upper-class.

Let's face it. Most of us came from a hard-working lower to middle class background at a genetic coding level. Now we're talking about

hundreds of thousands of dollars, millions of dollars, buying proper-
ties in exotic places and traveling the world and doing our business
from a laptop. There is a very
strong program that says, "And
who the hell do you think you
are—a rich person or something?" I can hear the
voice in the back of your
head cutting you down,
holding you back and
keeping you small in your
finances.

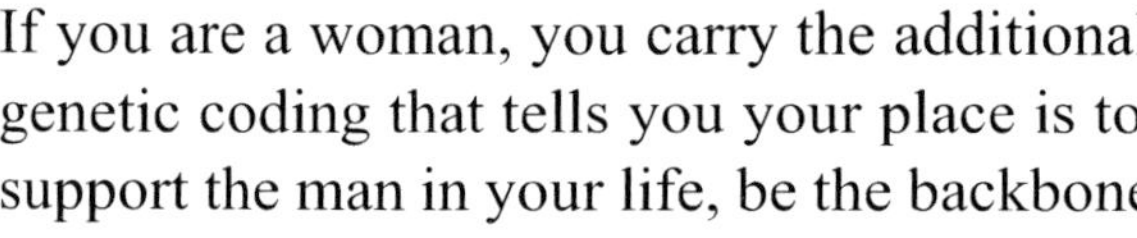

If you are a woman, you carry the additional
genetic coding that tells you your place is to
support the man in your life, be the backbone
of the family, be silent, submissive, subservient and hard-working.
You do all the labor and the man will make money. Your primary role
is to support the man and make sure that he looks good and is successful, which will in turn bring pride to you and to your family name. If
this sounds like something out of an old history book, it's not. This
kind of genetic coding has shown up in my own life and in my clients'
lives. It's frighteningly real.

Women, you really need to release and let go, at a DNA and cellular
level, the belief that a man will look after you, that you don't want to
dirty your hands with money, it's not up to you to look after yourself
financially, it's a man's job, you can't earn more money than your
husband, father, or male partner, and that it is wrong, unspiritual, or
not nice to earn money and lots of it. Those are real beliefs that you
are holding onto at a subconscious level, and until you let them go,
your financial success will always be limited and riddled with guilt.
We all need to release these strong limiting beliefs around money,
because money is important and necessary in both our lives and in
making a massive difference in the world.

But there's more.

          Getting Off the Merry-Go-Round

Chapter Sixty-Three...

Past lives have also had a tremendous impact on our financial success—or lack thereof. As I discussed, every single thought, belief, event and word has been filed into our Subconscious Mind at some level. When disastrous things happen to us, we file those events with a big red flag that says, "This is important."

We've probably had many lifetimes with a degree of wealth and lots of good experiences. However, just like in this lifetime, I bet that if I asked you what experiences you remember most vividly around any one thing, negative experiences would jump up pretty quickly.

Let's try it.

Think of money. What experience comes to mind right now? Is it the feeling when you had money and could buy anything you wanted, or was it the feeling that there's never enough, the credit cards are full, the debt is mounting, you're worried about retirement and old age because you are not prepared for it, or something similar? Those files coming up are the files that are running your financial show. The most predominant file that comes up for me is "I earn more than I spend." The second file is, "I desire more money" and I literally feel an excitement in my abdominal brain even writing about money.

What about you? I can honestly tell you that I had a lot of crap to release around money, and it took some time for me to get to this point. For a long time I would come up with what seemed like a bottomless pit of beliefs around money, beliefs that were holding me back. I promise you that if I can get to financial prosperity in my life with all the stuff I was attached to, so can you. Just notice. Not noticing is like pretending you don't have cancer by not going for the CAT scan. It doesn't change the fact that you have cancer—it simply limits your ability to deal with the situation and potentially rectify it. So look at this area without shame, embarrassment, or frustration, because these are simply beliefs that you have picked up along the journey, beliefs that you finally are capable of letting go of now that you are aware of them. If I had been able to go "shopping" for my beliefs in the "What I Want to Believe in this Lifetime" store, I probably would have picked at a conscious level very different beliefs from those I inherited, both from other people and from past lives.

So back to past lives. What effect are they having on your finances? Possibly lots. Probably tons. If you were wealthy in a past life and your children were kidnapped and held ransom because of your wealth, what information do you think you have in your file on wealth? "Wealth is dangerous. My family will suffer for my wealth. Something bad will happen to my kids." I have had clients who, after hearing about a past life in a session with me, have exclaimed, "That explains why I have this underlying feeling that if I have money, something awful would happen to my kids. Now I understand!"

Suppose that in a past life, while acquiring wealth, you acquired a terrible disease from the stress or even died. What is the file around wealth? "Creating wealth is stressful to my health. You get sick when you get wealthy. Wealth = death." How excited do you think your team is about going after wealth with that red flag waving in your Subconscious Mind? Right—about as excited as having your finger-nails pulled out one by one.

So if you notice that every time you start to move toward outrageous success or tremendous wealth, you get sick, or you get scared that you will get sick, this very well may be a program that is running your file around money.

Perhaps in a past life you lost your family because you were always away, earning money. Your wife left you, your kids didn't know you, and all of your hard work to produce wealth to benefit your family backfired on you. That can leave you with a really sour taste in your mouth around having wealth. You could have been very successful, a well-known philanthropist, a leader in the business community, but something bad happened, like a downturn in the economy, a business partnership that went south, or a literal disaster such as a fire or vandalism, war or natural disaster. Along with the wealth went the reputation, the honor and respect, replaced by scorn, ridicule, contempt or pity. Again, your Subconscious Mind pulls up the file for wealth every time you talk about it, envision it, plan for it or go after it, sees what's attached, and says, "I don't want to be hated and sick, have my family torn apart, or put my loved ones in danger! Nope, cancel that plan." In working with hundreds and hundreds of clients on their financial issues, I have seen how real this is—and I know that at an intuitive level, you are realizing this too.

Clear unhelpful beliefs around money in this lifetime and all past lives because they are affecting you.

Just Note:

- Are you able to earn a certain level of money and then it stops, dries up or disappears?

- Is there a comfort level you hit before hell breaks loose with your finances?

- What file comes up in your mind when I say the words, "wealth, rich or money" to you?

Chapter Sixty-Four...

With a topic as top-of-mind as money, I'm sure you won't be surprised that Tribal Mentality beliefs around money are numerous. One day while in the lab with God, I asked to be given all the Tribal Mentality beliefs around money. I took notes for hours. But I believe that you need to be aware of these beliefs because you have picked many of them up without even being aware of them. So here are some Tribal Mentality beliefs around money:

- $ Critical of it
- $ Don't trust it
- $ Suspicious of people with it
- $ Depressed about it
- $ Angry at it
- $ Want it, but avoid doing what it takes to have it
- $ Beat yourself up for not having it
- $ Use it as an excuse to not step into your godpower
- $ Blame God for you not having it
- $ Afraid of its power
- $ Think it needs to be a struggle
- $ Difficult to get
- $ Difficult to hold onto
- $ A fluke if you do get it
- $ Embarrassing if you have it
- $ Embarrassing if you don't have it
- $ Afraid of responsibility of having it

- $ Things will happen, and the uncertainty of what that looks like is scary
- $ Betrayed by people who have it
- $ Don't know what to do with it
- $ Too many rules and regulations around money
- $ Resets your boundaries
- $ Comfort zone changes
- $ Afraid of compromise to get it
- $ Afraid of compromise to keep it
- $ Selfish to have money
- $ Have to compete for it
- $ There's not enough of it
- $ Self-centered to have it
- $ Angry at what money can do
- $ Discipline needed to manage it
- $ Have to make decisions about it
- $ No agreement on it
- $ Money = status
- $ Money = power
- $ Money buys sex
- $ Money buys comfort
- $ Money determines your priorities in life
- $ Money gives you freedom to play and let go of control
- $ Uncomfortable with the freedom
- $ Feelings of guilt and shame
- $ Money is a private thing—not open

$ Scary to have money to live your passion

$ No money—feel trapped

$ Too much money = loss of independence

$ Family will become more demanding

$ If you have money, you no longer fit in with the Tribe

$ Fear of sacrifice to have it and keep it

$ Fear of change

$ Fear of success

$ Fear of failure

$ Sacrifice identity for money

$ Scrutinized for motives

$ Have to be all that you can be when you have money—
live life large

$ Will have to trust yourself with money

$ Able to pursue your dreams and ambitions

$ What will others think

$ You need a well-paying job to have money

$ Fear of rejection

$ Need to be frugal and miserly to have money

$ Being rich is dangerous

$ You'll become indulgent

$ You'll get spoiled

$ You'll be bored

$ Opportunities will open, and that's scary

$ Fear of others' approval, or lack of it

$ Like the drama of having no money

$ Ability to plan future—out of survival mode

$ Too much work

$ I don't know how

$ I'm ignorant about money

$ I don't know enough

$ It's not spiritual to have money

$ I can't do anything without money

$ If I have money, people will be fake around me

$ The gold diggers will only like me for my money

$ Money is bad

$ Money is tainted

$ Women don't earn as much money as men

As you can see from this long list, there are a lot of beliefs around money, many of them contradictory. Our beliefs don't have to make sense or even match. That's what makes us such interesting creatures! You can believe if you have no money, you feel trapped. Yet, at the same time, there may be a fear if you make lots of money, you will lose your independence because of all the responsibility. You may be excited about being able to do good things with money and at the same time, think that everybody will come out of the woodwork to take your money from you. You can want to be able to express your creativity, do things, go places and yet you're afraid you'll be seen as spoiled or indulgent.

Do you see how confusing it gets?

When you look at those beliefs, it's no wonder you don't have the money you really want. I suggest you go through this list and check off the ones that really resonate with you. Release them because they aren't working—I'm sure you have noticed! Add more that come to your mind and let them go.

Watch how you speak about money. If you use words like "dirty money," "rich bitch" or the like, notice that. I remember playing Robert Kiyosaki's board game *Cash Flow* with some people. One woman kept on saying every time another woman did well at a deal, "rich bitch." She didn't ever remember saying it when I later brought it to her attention as perhaps a reason why she was struggling financially.

Two other people celebrated their non-involvement in joint ventures to make money and literally high-fived each other as if they were making the "right" move by NOT getting involved in making money. Interesting—because neither of those people has a penny to her name. So if you watch a show on budgeting, notice whether you guffaw at it and make fun of the people on the show, are disrespectful, even in a joking way, or on the other hand, whether are saying to your team, "If there's anything here that would help us create financial freedom, please notice it, because I love having money and lots of it." These Tribal Mentality beliefs are insidiously woven into movies, books, advertising, the media and every other avenue in life, and our bank balance is a direct result of them without us even knowing it. It's time to change that, so let go of limiting, disrespectful and disempowering beliefs around money.

To Do...

Go through the list and see what resonates with you physically, emotionally and mentally. Don't just dismiss a belief because it feels stupid, silly or unreasonable. Then release those beliefs at a DNA and cellular level.

If you want more help on dealing with money issues, check out www.anamazinglifenow.com for my CD on money.

Chapter Sixty-Five...

I have a very fun game for you and your family. Pick a word—any word—and notice what pops up immediately for you. Money (dirty). Sex (bad). Love (dangerous). Play (guilty). Those are the files that are running your life. You may want to change some, add to others and keep some.

You can follow where the files lead. Think of something, then quietly watch what thoughts come into your mind. You may think "millionaire," then watch what comes up and let the sequence continue. There will be one. Perhaps it will be "impossible," "unlikely," "never," or the name of a famous millionaire you like or don't approve of. Where it ends is the conclusion you are coming to. You may or may not like the conclusion.

Purge the files you don't like by asking your Subconscious Mind to rewrite them. A conversation may look something like this: "Subconscious Mind, please remove the file that money is dirty. Replace it with the file that money is necessary, money is fun, money is easy to get, easy to keep, easy to have. Thank you." Believe it or not, the Subconscious Mind will respond.

Now I highly recommend you notice the emotions that come up with the belief that money is dirty. Those emotions may be embarrassment, shame, guilt, doubt, disdain, fear, discouragement, depression, terror, bad, unspiritual or whatever you feel. Clear those emotions as well, at a DNA and cellular level, because those emotions are linked to the file that money is dirty. You may be quite fascinated at what comes up for you, and it very well may explain why your life looks like it does in the area of money, relationships, sex, career, marriage and family. Check in frequently, as the files will change as you do your work in clearing old files and bringing in new beliefs.

Chapter Sixty-Six...

You've probably noticed I have mentioned the word "unspiritual" several times in these chapters around money. It's because religion has had a tremendous impact on people's view on money. I know from spending most of my life studying the Bible that I had drilled into me, "You cannot slave for two Masters. You cannot slave for God and for riches." To my young mind, that said, "I can't be rich if I am going to work for God." The next file linked to that was "I must work for God if I want to be saved." Hence right there the association is God = saved, riches = die.

Do you see how insidiously these beliefs come into our life? We make assumptions and connections that aren't necessarily true, but our Subconscious Mind doesn't reason—it simply files the thought, belief and the emotion. What emotion came up with that scripture? The fear of displeasing God. So now fear is linked to money.

Many people will say, "But that's simply not true! There are lots of stories in the Bible about wealthy people." I know those stories well, believe me—and a closer look will reveal the ways in which those stories are told, and to what purpose.

Abraham, who was called a "friend of God" was a wealthy man. The Bible says he owned cattle and sheep and fields and was well known for his abundance. So what happened to Abraham? God told him that as an example of his faith, he needed to leave his home city of Ur, travel and live in tents. Then he later was asked to sacrifice his only son, Isaac. While his beloved child was on an altar, he raised the knife to kill him, and God stopped him and said, "Now I know you're faithful."

What is that all about? Leaving his home, living in tents and obeying God up until then wasn't enough?

So what is the file that gets filed with that story? To serve God, even wealthy people must make sacrifices, lose their wealth and have their loved ones taken away. Not a particularly empowering file, with all the emotions of fear, terror and anger.

Job is another well known wealthy man, the "richest of all the Orientals." Job suffered one catastrophe after another, losing all of his livestock and family, seeing his friends ridicule him and having his health fell apart. After all of the suffering of Job, he eventually was rewarded with double the livestock and more children. The file is: You have to suffer in order to be rewarded and the file linked to that is: Money = suffering.

And need I even mention Matthew 19:24? "It is easier for a camel to go through the eye of a needle than for a rich man to enter the kingdom of God."

Yes, you will indeed find scriptures that talk about prosperity and abundance, money is for a protection, and other positive texts, but the negative stories of suffering have a far greater emotional impact than a few nice words. The majority of religions have been advocates of poverty, ignorance and fear. Guilt has been a powerful weapon of control. Thank God, times are changing and we are seeing some shift in viewpoint, but we have a long way to go to releasing the indoctrination of poverty files in the masses today. Look with an open mind at what your religion or spiritual beliefs teach about money, because they are having a tremendous effect on your bank account.

Ask Yourself:

What beliefs have I picked up about money and God?

Please don't assume you don't have any because you most likely do, from either genetic coding, Tribal Mentality, your parents or a past life.

Chapter Sixty-Seven...

Have you noticed the abundance in the world? Living on a beachfront in Mexico, there's a lot of sand and a lot of water out there. There is nothing chintzy about God. We don't have one kind of food, but an overflow of food with a wonderful variety. There isn't one kind of insect either (what a shame!), but hundreds of different sizes, shapes and colors. Everything in the Universe is in abundance.

When I think about any new belief that I want to adopt, I always go back to the abundance of nature. This is very much in line with the subject of money. Are you in a place of abundance or lack? Just as there are always people running around like Chicken Little waiting for the sky to fall, there are people who always see the lack. Are you one of them? If so, it's time to change that, to move out of a place of fear, doubt and guilt. If you are not experiencing abundance, no matter what you think you think, the proof of the pudding is in the eating. What are your results? This isn't a judgment—this is a fact of life. Put black dye in the water and you will end up with black water. Not a judgment—a fact. There is no difference in what is showing up in your life.

Lack mentality produces lack in your life. Abundance mentality produces abundance in your life. Which have you chosen? This can be a hard one for many people because you don't see where the lack is coming from. Listen to what you say. Do you say things like, "There's never enough money, there's never enough time, I always run out of money, I don't have any friends, or I'm afraid if I do such-and-such, there won't be enough." Everything, from the sand on the seashore to the stars, are in abundance. The more we mimic nature, the happier we are. Think abundance. Release all files around lack. Let go of the belief that there isn't enough. There's more than enough of everything we need. Right now, more than ever, we need to stay in a place of abundance so our team can create that abundance for ourselves and others.

Ask Yourself:

- Do I think of abundance or lack?

- What do I talk about?

- Do I focus on what I have or what I don't have?

- Am I generous or chintzy?

- Do I immediately think of what I can't do, have or be, or do I appreciate all the good in my life?

Chapter Sixty-Eight...

You may be sleeping with the enemy because you are your own worst enemy.

Could this possibly be referring to you? You don't need to be beat up, punched down or pulled apart like a master baker working bread dough needing to rise. You do a fine job yourself of tearing down your own self-esteem and self-worth.

Jane had done such a remarkable job of finding what she really loved to do, had earned money doing it, and was feeling on top of the world, but a few weeks later, she wasn't sounding so great. What had happened? Like many of us, she had written goals for the first three months of the year, and when she didn't meet them, she started beating herself up. Feeling completely inadequate, useless and unforgiving of herself, she was on a rampage of self-destruction. Jane also felt wicked, as if she had disappointed God in her pathetic attempt at life.

Whoa, whoa, whoa! An hour later, we had chewed the fat together on this one and spit out quite a different version of her existence. A big secret to living a life without fear, doubt and guilt is to remember that you are human. "Human" means that you make mistakes. It's all part of the game. It comes with the package. You can't get away from the fact that a big part of the humanness of us is that we make mistakes. Period. Not open to discussion or negotiation. Can we make fewer mistakes, less serious mistakes, smaller mistakes? Absolutely! But we will make mistakes.

Would you look at a two-year-old and expect him to make a five-course meal for 100 people? Have you asked your ten-year-old to read *War and Peace* and write a 5,000-word essay on it? Crazy you say. Of course it is and you know exactly where I am going with this one. It is just as ridiculous for a Supreme Power to expect perfection from humans. The word "sin" in Classical Greek simply meant "missing the mark of perfection." No kidding. So the word "sin" is not some awful thing that only happens to the worst of people. We're all sinners because we ALL miss the mark of perfection. Of course we do. We're human!

The only thing we can change is our perspective and emotions around making those mistakes. If you praise children, have you noticed what happens? They perk up, their shoulders go back and their head is a little straighter. Many times they respond by going above and beyond what you asked them. Chastise them severely, especially when it is unjustly, and notice how their shoulders slump, their head is bowed and they look like deflated balloons. They get quiet and pensive. It's because a child can't understand why you are getting so angry at them when they are doing what is natural. That little soul is thinking, "Wow, they're tough down here. I'm human, I make mistakes. Why does it have to be such a big deal?" We often beat ourselves up because that is our program from infancy. Our parents beat us up, either physically, emotionally or mentally, just as they beat themselves up, and we have carried on the tradition.

Let's release the need to punish ourselves, shall we, for what is perfectly natural—being imperfect. I am perfectly imperfect. I am really, really, really good at it. I've had lots of practice and I do it well. We all do. That takes all the pressure off. God doesn't expect perfection from us either, believe it or not.

Does that mean you can just let things slide, never improve or work on yourself? No, it does not. But deep down, you don't want to do that anyways so it really isn't an issue. You want peace, you desire happiness, and you would love more joy in your life. Otherwise, you would never have picked up this book nor done any of the other things along the way on your personal, spiritual, professional and financial journey. It's in the very core of our DNA to improve, evolve and grow.

Joanna was beating herself up for not being like Donald Trump. The Donald only sleeps a few hours, never takes a vacation and drives himself constantly. Good for The Donald! So what? If you're feeling guilty because you sleep eight hours and take a vacation, if you believe you should be making more sacrifices in your life to be better, do better, and stay on that crazy merry-go-round of "I'm not good enough just the way I am," you are depriving yourself of a tremendous amount of joy.

Some may be fine on four hours of sleep. Good for them. Let me tell you, if I tried to make the sacrifice of only sleeping four hours a night, there'd be a sacrifice all right. I'd probably kill someone! It won't work for me. And it quite honestly doesn't work for many people who are trying to do it.

Why not look at it this way: You can sit on the thorn in life, find all the negative, beat yourself up, criticize everyone else and hate it. Or you can make a shift and smell the rose instead. The thorn or the rose? Your choice. But if you think you're living with a thorn stuck up your rear because God expects that of you, that is entirely your story—not God's.

Let it go—there are much better stories to hold on to.

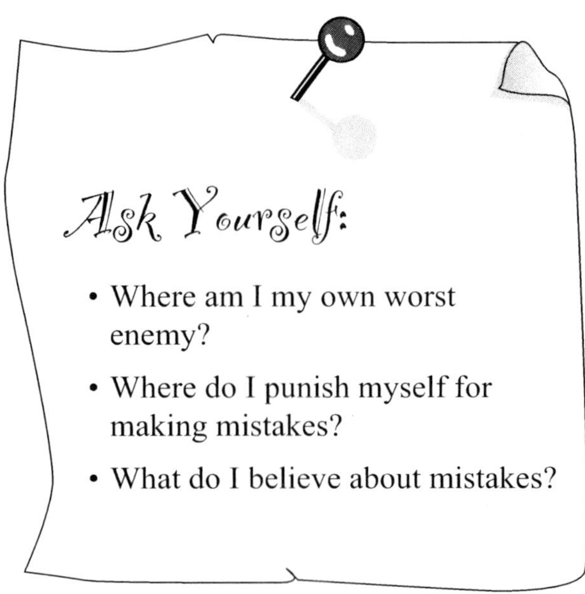

- Where am I my own worst enemy?
- Where do I punish myself for making mistakes?
- What do I believe about mistakes?

Chapter Sixty-Nine

When am I going to talk about your ego? Doesn't your ego negatively affect your life? Don't you need to be on guard against it?

Ego is made out to be this big black ugly monster that makes us appear to be "not nice people." You can decide what you want about the ego, but I never talk about it because I don't believe from my sessions in the lab with God that we even have an ego as it is commonly understood—something inside of us that controls us to do evil. I think we have programs that create triggers, responses and reactions to situations. It's that simple.

So someone is boasting about an accomplishment. We would normally identify that person as having an ego. I would say that person doesn't feel good about him or herself at a subconscious or soul level and is looking for recognition and importance. Identify why they don't feel good about themselves and give them the recognition they probably deserve but don't know how to get because of their upbringing. Suddenly you no longer have an "ego problem."

We feel hurt because someone says something mean and we react. People will say our ego was hurt. In fact, the comment triggered a program, belief or emotion filed in your Subconscious Mind that was based on fear, anger or some other negative emotion. Resolve that memory and you won't react that way the next time around.

We all have an innate need to be important. Of course we do. That's not ego—that's our divinity or our "godness" coming out. Unfortunately, it doesn't always show up dressed in a black tuxedo with tails, but rather shows up in mismatched clothes that smell of bad B.O. As we find the balance between knowing that we are the most important person in the world and caring about others, the apple cart is sometimes upset. You see, we know in the very core of our DNA that we deserve the best—we have God/Eternal Within the Body written in our very DNA. We are made in God's image. We get our own perfection at a core level. Yet we are dealing with the imperfection of our flesh and blood at the same time. It makes for a challenging walk on the tightrope of life.

At times we say or do things that don't reflect the godness within each and every one of us. Sometimes we fall short of our divinity—grossly short. Recall the meaning of sin—missing the mark of perfection. However, as we release the programs that we don't feel loved, appreciated, important, valued, respected and honored, we also need less assurance that we really are okay. We don't need to blow our own horn in public when everyone would like some silence. We don't find ourselves reacting to every comment with criticism and a harsh tongue because we are at peace with ourselves and the world.

Someone once told me that ego was an acronym for Edging God Out. I like that! That works for me. Ego is not a bad thing any more than it is a good thing—ego is just what I call the outward response or reaction to something that triggers an emotion, belief or program in us. Every response or reaction probably doesn't quite emulate God in his perfection. Everything we say does edge God out some way, somehow. Which makes sense. We are not God. We are made in God's image and we have God's magnificent qualities in our makeup, in our very DNA, but we are not God and so we will not act like God. Rather than be concerned, upset and focused on our ego from a negative standpoint, why not let go of more of the fear, doubt, guilt and need to be more important than the next person?

As you let go of the programming and beliefs that foster low self-esteem and unworthiness, you will edge God out less and less. You still may horrify or shock yourself once in a while when you have a negative reaction to something that comes up in your life, but just recognize what got triggered and then let it go. It's nothing to be ashamed of, to be embarrassed about, or to feel guilty over. It's part of the refining process of who you are as you move into greater and greater power, part of the growing process as you move into greater and greater love. It is simply part of the package of being a human. So accept the opportunities to see what needs to be healed as a gift, a precious treasure, and not as something you need to beat yourself up over. Apologize, make amends, do what is necessary to make right the wrong and get on with life. It's much more peaceful, joyful and loving to feel compassion and understanding for yourself and others rather than seeing the ego, the evil, the Satan in people.

Look for the God in everyone including yourself, and you'll be amazed at the goodness you find. It's really quite remarkable.

Ask Yourself:

- When has someone told me my ego was getting in the way?

- When have I had a reaction that felt like it came up and out of me and I had no control over it?

- What triggers me into the emotions of fear, anger, hurt, defensiveness or bitchiness?

- Do I feel I am important?

- Do I believe I am good enough?

Chapter Seventy...

So you're on the merry-go-round of dieting, being overweight or even obese. The only God you may be feeling like is a big round Buddha! You've done it all—every diet, every program, every book, yet you're heavier than when you started. You're now depressed and a lot more broke than you were before. What went wrong? Weight is a complex issue because we have a lot vested in our weight right down to our choice of mate and our survival. No joking!

What do you believe about weight? Your answer is affecting your weight more than you think. When I fell in love with Greg, I started to gain weight. I realized ten pounds later that it was my way of testing his love. My father had always been very critical of my mother's weight and as his three daughters grew up, we were very aware that slim was acceptable, fat was not. So would Greg really love me if I was overweight? Would he pick on me, be critical or judgmental? At a subconscious level, I realize that I was waiting for his condemnation. I had been programmed to expect it. I also understood clearly that as my father did not tolerate being overweight, my weight was a way of saying to Dad, "I'm a big girl now. I'll do what I please and you won't control me."

Many of us have a lot of anger around our weight issues. Dad or a big brother may have tormented us, school mates or even sisters may have teased and ridiculed us about our weight. In our defiance of their control, we now say: "I'll weigh what I want," and so we do. In other words, we cut off our nose to spite our face. Let go of all the anger you have towards your family about weight, your culture regarding weight and yourself about your weight. It's much easier to release the weight when you come from a place of peace rather than being pissed off.

There are all sorts of Tribal Mentality beliefs concerning weight. "It's hard to lose weight. As you get older, you naturally gain weight. You can't eat anything you like when you lose weight. You need help from someone or somebody to lose weight. Skinny people are healthy. Fat people aren't." We definitely have a Tribal Mentality belief that while a woman is looking for a man, she is expected to be slim and trim, but once he's caught, she doesn't need to be careful about her weight any longer. She has other priorities, such as bearing children and raising a family, so it's acceptable for her to gain weight.

The media has made losing weight a major issue and a massive moneymaker. It has us convinced that losing weight is so difficult, so challenging and so complicated that you cannot do it alone. I'll never forget hearing Loretta LaRoche, an incredible comedian, joking about weight problems. In her sardonic way, LaRoche said, "The solution to weight problems is to eat less and move more." The audience of more than 2,000 women roared with laughter because they knew she was absolutely right. We've taken a very simple issue and made it into an incredibly complicated situation that tells the Subconscious Mind, "This must be difficult. All she talks about is food and what she can't eat, what she can't have, how many calories there are, how much fat she is getting. We need to prioritize this issue that weight is complicated."

Replace that file with the file that being the perfect weight for you is simple. Genetic coding also plays a role in weight issues because having some extra weight in many cultures is seen as a good thing necessary for survival. A woman who is too skinny would not be a good choice of mate as she wouldn't be able to bear children easily or work hard on the farm and might even be an embarrassment to her husband because she would give the appearance of there not being enough food to fatten her up. With disease rampant, famines prevalent and life physically demanding, having extra weight was an important characteristic. There was also the cold. Fat insulates and helps keep you warm in the cold, harsh winters.

The problem with all of that genetic coding is that famine to date is not an issue where obesity is a problem, diseases like the bubonic plague no longer run rampant, and we sit on our butts most of the day at computers. We are a far cry today from working in the field from morning to night, hoeing, plowing and harvesting. And the last time I checked, there was central heating in most of the world where people are the fattest. So the genetic coding needs to be deleted because times have changed and the program that's running is way out-of-date. It's also a very strong genetic coding in many cultures that as women get older, they are expected to gain weight and become more matronly and less sexually desirable. It's still in our genes that the young women need to procreate and therefore must be sexually attractive. It's like the over-45 crowd needs to move over and make room for the young who will propagate the species. Being in that age group, that was genetic coding I made sure to let go of as soon as I understood it!

Do past lives also affect weight? You bet! While clearing issues around weight in my life, I got a very clear visual of a roly-poly Indian man with a large belly, dressed in beautiful gold garb with gold bangles on his arms. He was obviously very wealthy and very fat. I realized that from a past life experience, I associated fat with wealth. That is a very common belief. And think about it, if you see someone starving to death, malnourished or skin and bones, you automatically associate that condition with poverty. Wealthy = fat, skinny = poor.

If you have had a past life where you dealt with starvation issues, you will feel this need to eat like there is no tomorrow. Stuff your face almost to the point of making yourself sick because you have no idea if there will be food once this is gone. If that's you, you know exactly the feeling I am talking about. You probably have had a past life around starvation, and it's probably a fairly highly charged lifetime. Death from starvation is a very, very painful way to die. You have remembered it only too well. So let go of any beliefs, at a DNA and cellular level, that you are starving to death, that food is in scarce supply, that you need to eat everything today because there may not be any food tomorrow, and that you need to store up, stock up and prepare yourself for starvation. There are several emotional reasons why you are retaining the weight. Fear of losing your survival ability. Fear of dying. Fear of being cold. Fear of not being able to attract a mate. Fear of not being able to work hard enough. Anger at someone or something that implied that fat people are stupid or ugly (you will be proving them wrong and YOU right at some level). Anger at yourself for something you did (punishing yourself). A belief that you don't deserve to be slim, healthy, or attractive.

For many women, there's a very deep, dark reason why you are overweight. Let's go there now.

Ask Yourself:

- Are you happy with your weight?
- Have you resigned yourself about where you're at with your weight goals?
- What were your family beliefs around weight, love and acceptance?
- Were you teased or ridiculed about weight as a child?
- What file comes up for you when I say "weight, fat or food"?

To Do:

Check the website www.anamazinglifenow.com for resources on weight from myself and other experts.

Relax and know that you can be at your ideal weight.

Chapter Seventy-One...

A buse is common—much more common than we want to believe. I deal with clients every week who have experienced abuse at some level—physical, emotional, mental and sexual. It's at pandemic proportions and has taken a heavy toll on the recipients' ability to truly live lives of peace, joy, love and prosperity.

Sexual abuse is one of those things that deeply impacts a woman. I have dealt with many men who have been sexually abused also, so it is not only a female issue, but when it comes to weight, I have found that women will use weight to protect themselves as they get older. I know this is not pleasant, but imagine a little girl being sexually molested by an older brother, a father, an uncle, a religious leader, a school teacher, or some other authority figure. She feels powerless, helpless and completely out of control. She learns very quickly that her boundaries are not respected and that she is vulnerable. What she knows in the very core of her soul is that this is wrong, yet it is happening to her and she is feeling a tremendous number of emotions, including fear, pain—and even pleasure.

Imagine having the father she loves telling her she is special or that she is Daddy's girl as he touches her inappropriately. What a hornet's nest of emotions that stirs up! Feelings of guilt, shame, embarrassment, anger, helplessness, danger, pleasure, love, nurturing, importance and doubt. Sexual abuse is a complicated issue from an emotional point of view but having dealt with hundreds of variations on the same theme – the emotions of fear, guilt, anger and shame are universal. When it comes to later dealings with men, women who have been abused, either through inappropriate sexual behavior or actual sexual penetration, often want to be unattractive to men so they are safe. Remember how important safety is to your team. They will do everything and anything to be safe, including being overweight and unattractive. If they weigh more than many men, women can feel powerful and in control, as if they can throw their weight around and show him who's boss. "Nobody will ever take advantage of me again" is another strong program that runs rampant. Protecting herself is a priority, and the men in her life will be seen as "the enemy" even if they were not the original perpetrator.

So if you are dealing with a weight issue and sexual abuse has been in your past, please know that this is most probably contributing to your weight situation. Get professional help to deal with the abuse. It is affecting you in many ways—financially, sexually, healthwise— and is damaging your self-esteem. Your creativity, your sexuality and your finances are all issues that are related at an energetic level, and when one is blocked, they are all affected. Let go at a DNA and cellular level that you are responsible, to blame or in any way guilty for what happened to you. The child who is sexually abused is simply NEVER, EVER, EVER to blame for what happened and you need to know that in the very core of your DNA. You are loved, you are honored, you are valued and you can be healed of the after-effects of sexual abuse. It is nothing to be ashamed, embarrassed or guilty about. It is a memory you can release along with all of the emotions attached to it. You deserve to do that for yourself.

So is there anything physical about getting off the merry-go-round of weight we need to discuss? There actually is. It's the simplest part.

Chapter Seventy-Two...

Your body, that important member of the team, doesn't necessarily see weight loss as a priority. When I had my miraculous health comeback because of algae back in 1996, I became a distributor of the product I believed saved my life. People would say to me, "Will it help me lose weight?" As I learned about the intelligence of the oldest food on the planet, my answer was always, "Your body will deal with priorities once it gets the nutrition of the algae into it. However, if you are about to die of a heart attack, your body will use the algae to fix your heart because it won't matter how fat you are if you're dead. You'll just need a bigger coffin."

They got it. Your body needs to be in good physical condition to release the weight. So just as I saw those frayed wires that were the nervous system and explained to the medical doctor at an appointment with me that as long as the nervous system was strung out, burned out, and feeling fried, the body could not really deal with the weight situation in a safe and long-term manner, I'm telling you that the body needs to be healthy to deal with the weight. It doesn't mean that sick people can't lose weight, because they can, but I am talking about healthy, sustained weight release. You need to be giving your body the nutrition to fix and repair, and then it will get around to weight release. Otherwise, have you noticed you feel driven back to the fridge, opening it and staring at it like something should be happening? It's your precious body saying, "I don't have the nutrition I need to do my work. Maybe if I drive you back to the fridge or cupboard, you will find something that has nutritional value for me to use to repair your heart, your brain, your liver and your nerves."

We have reached the point of eating for all the wrong reasons—that this or that food makes me feel happy, safe, loved, peaceful, nurtured, comforted or relaxed—instead of "I need to eat because I need

Vitamins A, B, C, D, E, iron, potassium, and everything else I need to maintain a healthy body." We even refer to foods that make us feel good as "comfort foods." We've all gone to the fridge fairly soon after eating a meal as if there was something missing. You may feel like you need something sweet, but what your body may need is a vitamin or a vital mineral you're not getting in your regular diet. That's why it's really important to provide your body with what it needs from a nutritional standpoint so it's not having to rob Peter to pay Paul! Otherwise your body is frantic, panicked or stressed simply trying to keep you alive!

Then on top of all that, you think it should lose weight when it's having a hard time just functioning without the proper materials. You'd never expect someone to build you a house without cement, wood, wiring, tools, and a thousand other necessary items the contractor requires. Why would you expect your body to repair you, rebuild you and keep you in top shape without the components that you need at a physical level? When you deal with the emotional issues around weight from a genetic coding level, all past lives, all emotions, programs and beliefs around weight, COMBINED with the physical issues, then you are well on your way to creating a happy, healthy body that automatically knows its ideal weight.

Ask Yourself:

- What am I doing to support my weight goals?

- Do I make wise food choices?

- Do I eat regularly?

- Do I drink adequate water?

- Do I move enough to utilize the food I eat?

- What unhealthy habit would I like to release
  around weight?

Chapter Seventy-Three...

One of the areas left to deal with is relationships. I work with many clients who would find their lives much more joyful, peaceful and loving if they just had that someone special to share it with. Even if that's not you, you may wish to improve your current relationship or find a new one. As we now understand, the Subconscious Mind is constantly associating thoughts with files with emotions. So for example, if I say "men," the Subconscious Mind pulls the file "abusive." But it doesn't end there. That file on abusive is linked to another file which may be life-threatening, painful, terrifying, or angry. That file is linked to another file which says "stay away." And women will wonder why they simply can't meet a man or find a suitable relationship. Do you see what happens? That sequence happens so quickly and so unconsciously, it is frightening. You come to conclusions all the time about things—right or wrong, good or bad, and you live by those conclusions, many of which you aren't even aware of.

As I wrote in an earlier chapter, you can follow the files yourself. Think of something, then quietly watch what thoughts come into your mind. You may think "marriage," and then watch what comes up and let the sequence continue. There will be a sequence, and where it ends is the conclusion you are coming to. You may or may not like the conclusion. Release and let go of the files you don't like.

I will often say to a Subconscious Mind: "Subconscious Mind—New File." Then I state the new belief and attach the desired emotions to the file. Stating a new belief WITHOUT the emotion won't hold because it is the emotions that hold all the charge. So if you want a new file on men for example, think of the new belief and state it out loud. For example: "I really love and trust men and have a wonderful relationship in my life." Now think of all the emotions that go along with that belief. Imagine the feeling of joy as you enjoy the benefits of a close companion, a life-partner, and the feelings of love as you envision romantic evenings and weekends, feel the closeness and the intimacy of having someone really love you unconditionally, feel how special you are to that person and let the love flow through you like water through a hose. Bask in the trust and confidence you feel as you entwine your life with your man, the precious giggles and the shared secrets.

Get the idea?

Without the new belief and the emotions attached to it, there won't be anything to get your team excited about. Get excited, and now we're talking. In every area of relationships, from meeting someone who really values and respects you to feeling intelligent, worthy, sexy and beautiful as you grow that relationship, look at the files that are operating in your Subconscious Mind. Your parent's relationship and your previous relationships in this life and all past lives are having an effect on your current situation. I had to release a BIG hatred and distrust of men, a massive belief that "I didn't need any man in my life to tell me what to do" and an incredibly strong program that any man would screw up my finances, waste my time and ruin my life! I released them and have been in a most amazing relationship with the love of my life for 18 months. I know you can let go of these beliefs, programs and negative emotions too. True joy, peace and love in a relationship await you also. Promise!

Chapter Seventy-Four...

So what do you really want your five CEOs to do for you in a day? That's the question with which I end every first session with a client. I always start with your body, because quite honestly, without your body, our conversation about life here on earth ends fairly abruptly. I want you to see your body as a beautiful Rolls-Royce. It's gorgeous, sleek, shiny, expensive and precious. Every gadget, gizmo and doodad in that vehicle has been well thought through. It's been tested to a very high state of excellence. Words like "perfect," "wow," and "speechless!" are how you describe the ride in a Rolls-Royce. That's your body. If we actually knew all the gadgets, gizmos and doodads at work in our body every day, helping us to eat, breathe, sleep, digest and eliminate, we would probably be in much greater awe of who we are. And just as you wouldn't dream of hauling horse manure in your brand new Rolls-Royce, you wouldn't dream of putting the crap in your body that you do if you really got that one fact.

So let's begin by really honoring the body, the vehicle for life here on Earth and "home" to your conscious mind, Subconscious Mind, Spirit and Soul. It's worth honoring sooner rather than later, believe me. Your body's assignment is to let your team know what it needs. If it needs more rest, more nutrition, certain nutrition, more water or less stress, then it is your body's job to communicate that. It works very closely with the conscious mind and the Subconscious Mind in accomplishing all of the bodily functions automatically and in making conscious decisions about what you will eat and do, and how you will live your life.

Spirit is the next CEO I deal with, because Spirit is the fuel for this vehicle. It is what makes it move. Without the breath of life or Spirit, you're out of here. So Spirit's job is to keep you moving with the most power possible. I always ask it to remember two vital things. One is to remember where it came from. It came from that Universal Ocean of Spirit that is powerful—it created the Earth, Heavens and everything in them. Spirit moves mountains. It can do miracles in your life.

Secondly, remember it is still connected to that Universal Ocean of Spirit and it has access to all the knowledge that is available. It's like having a library card to the library of God. Spirit has access to unlimited knowledge, wisdom and power. That's the fuel that is operating your vehicle. This isn't some low-grade fuel that's mostly water and makes the vehicle sputter and stall. We're asking for the best quality fuel in the Universe. You deserve it, and it is available to you. You simply need to ask.

Subconscious Mind is the driver of this vehicle and always has been. You are driven by the programs and files stored in the Subconscious mind. So you haven't always had the best direction. It's now time to change that. I ask the Subconscious Mind to release all the sub-files for the work I have done with a client because there will be millions and millions of sub-files related to every single issue. I then ask it to do something incredibly important. As the Subconscious Mind has always just pulled the file with the highest charge—you know, the one with the little red flag waving screaming, "pick me, pick me, I'm the most important"—I ask it to instead always choose the most positive file it can find, even if it is a tiny little file way at the back of the bottom drawer.

Millions of times a second, your Subconscious Mind is searching for files. You see something—it connects to a file. You hear something—it connects to a file. You smell something—it connects to a file. We see, hear, smell, taste, and touch millions and millions of things each day and each one is connected to a file stored in the Subconscious Mind. I simply ask it to pull the most positive file related to every single thing it needs. It's fully capable of doing that—it just needs to be told and as we release the charge around the old beliefs and let them go, the files become more and more positive and easier to find and more emotionally charged with lots of good beliefs.

Soul is in the passenger seat. Your soul knows exactly what to do, why it's here, what needs to get done and how it wants it done. Your soul knows its reason for being here. Empowered with a team all heading toward the same goalpost, life can be accomplished so much smoother, easier and more graciously. Soul's job is to lead the team, to convey the mission to the troops and to get the job done. Once your soul is on track, it's amazing how much gentler life can be. Its job is to remember it has unlimited knowledge from all the past lives that it has lived. Your soul will have forgotten your past lives, but once reminded, it will pull experiences, knowledge, wisdom and expertise from all lifetimes to get the job done.

There is a vast wealth of knowledge and wisdom available to you between Spirit and Soul. Once you start using those resources, life can flow much more easily.

So what about our last CEO?

 *In Review:*

    BODY is the vehicle
    SPIRIT is the fuel
    SUBCONSCIOUS MIND is the driver
    SOUL is in the passenger's seat

Chapter Seventy-Five...

As for the Conscious Mind, I don't even put it in the vehicle. As medical doctors have discovered while doing surgery, it doesn't actually reside in our brain anyway. The job I give the Conscious Mind is to look after the logistics. So just as a travel agent may plan your trip, book the hotels, and suggest restaurants and places to see along the way, I let my Conscious Mind look after my physical needs at a very conscious level. The Subconscious Mind is dealing with the physical things I am not aware of such as how my heart beats, but the Conscious Mind can remind me of things that need to be done—who to phone for an appointment, who I need to call, and other very practical, logical details I need to deal with in a given day.

Perhaps you have noticed your mind feels quite full, overloaded and oftentimes overwhelmed. Perhaps you are doing a renovation on the house, working on growing a business, planning a move or buying a new vehicle. It feels like there are at least a million things to do. There probably aren't, but when you keep everything going around in your head, it's like a luggage carousel where you see the same 30 items over and over and over again, so you feel like there must be at least 300 or 3,000 or 30,000 items. Stop for a few minutes and write down on a piece of paper the things that are in your head. Someone once told me, "Your mind is not for storage—it's for processing," and she was absolutely right. Get the big pieces off your mind and let it do its job.

When I decided to move to Mexico, I had forty days to give notice, sell most of my belongings, pack up what I was keeping and put it into storage, pack to move to Mexico, leave the condo in excellent condition and organize all personal and business mail so I could leave the country. On top of that, I had sixty clients booked in those forty days—and it was over Christmas time! Most people would think, "Impossible, are you crazy? How stressful!" Do you know that I never felt stressed? It was quite remarkable to see everything fall into place. My conscious mind did the most amazing job of exactly the role I had given it—logistics. It reminded me of things I needed to do in a sequential manner, it gave me brilliant ideas on how to get it all done, and as I saw the list get shorter and shorter, it helped me remember small things that never made it on the list.

Your conscious mind is an amazing part of the team. We really don't appreciate how conscientious it can be about the details, without being overbearing, nagging and frantic. Part of my success was that I wrote stuff down so it wasn't all in my head. I emptied my head regularly and then went to work. I also fully expected my conscious mind to do its job—the job that it is here to do—to make my life easier from a logistical point of view. So get it out of your head and onto paper. You may never look at that paper again. You don't even need to check anything off. Just write it down. It works. I proved it under what could have been the most trying of circumstances.

As I conclude a session with a client, I have one important request of the Conscious Mind: that it asks its questions only once and then patiently waits. I assure it that either Spirit, Soul, Body or Subconscious Mind will get it the answer it needs in its perfect time and ask it to relax. This is how you too can get rid of that "mind frick" and "monkey mind" that may be controlling your life. My Conscious Mind does not natter at me, nag me, or irritate me. I see it as my Personal Assistant—and we have a great working relationship. Because I have released so much of the fear in my life, it does not operate from a place of fear, worry, or doubt, but feels confident in the team and where we are headed as a team. Your Conscious Mind never wanted to be in charge—that's not its role—but it does love the logistics. It feels appropriately safe in that position and consequently is very easy to get along with. I know this may seem hard to believe, but it is absolutely true.

You have a remarkable team and when they all work together in peace, love, joy and harmony, miracles happen. They really do.

Chapter Seventy-Six...

Some people are so afraid to get off their merry-go-rounds because they think that if they do (1) they will never get back on, and (2) life will change.

Amen to both!

Stop and think about this. Do you really, really, really love your life? Is your life so frickin' amazing that you can barely believe it? Are you living beyond your wildest dreams every single day? Have you had to come up with bigger dreams and goals because you've already done everything you ever wanted to do? No?

Well then what the heck are you worried about?

You really don't want to get back on the merry-go-round of too much to do, not enough time, never good enough, no money, stress, fat and poor health, do you? Please tell me no! Then you don't need to worry about never getting back on the craziness of spinning around in your life with that sickening, dizzying feeling that you are trapped and powerless. And YES, your life will change when you get off the merry-go-round and start changing your beliefs. It better! That's the whole point. Start laughing at your worries and fear that your life will change. Then do your work and let those nonsensical beliefs go at a DNA and cellular level. They are not serving you, bringing you love, joy, peace and prosperity.

What comes after the merry-go-round? When you get off a literal merry-go-round, you may feel a little dizzy at first. It may take a few minutes to get your footing, get grounded and feel normal. Maybe you have never been at what I call homeostasis or zero point, so "normal" can feel a bit weird at first. It may feel abnormal to operate from a place of joy, love, and peace instead of fear, doubt and guilt. You may feel surprised when you actually have money in your life rather than the usual scrimping and feeling of "never enough" that has predominated your entire life.

Relax – homeostasis is where your entire team wants to be. It's where you operate most fully mentally, emotionally, spiritually, physically and financially. It's where the magic happens.

One powerful exercise I do with clients is to "ground them." I believe you can actually do this once and stay grounded, but you can also do this as often as you feel necessary. You may wish to do this exercise standing up with both feet firmly planted on the ground.

Envision a white solid beam of light coming down from the Universe and entering you, starting about 6 to 8 inches above your head. See that beam of light entering your brain, coming down through the Third Eye in between your eyebrows, down through your throat and into your heart. From your heart it goes into your solar plexus or abdominal brain and then behind your belly button. At that point this beam of light divides into three prongs—one coming out between your legs, and then one beam of light going down each leg and coming out at the soles of your feet and straight into the center of the Earth. As it passes through your body, that beam of light permeates and enwraps every cell of your body with love, joy, peace and prosperity. It extends to the tips of your fingers. Every organ is wrapped in love. As you are connected from above to Father Sky and below to Mother Earth, you are grounded, protected and supported. You are linked from above to the very core of the Earth and attached to the support from below. Feel the love. Feel the peace. Feel the joy and relax. If ever you feel like you have come "undone," you can simply reach above your head about 6 to 8 inches and hook yourself back on to the Universe much like you would hook a plant hanger onto a ceiling hook. You will immediately feel connected again.

You deserve everything you can imagine, every dream, goal and vision you have for your life. William Arthur Ward said, "If you can imagine it, you can achieve it; if you can dream it, you can become it," and that is true. You are capable of everything you want. You have perhaps noticed throughout this book how many times I have used the word simple. I have done that on purpose. "It's very simple." "Pretty simple." "It's simple." I have used this word frequently so your five CEOs really get that it is doable and possible to do what I am suggesting. And honestly it is.

Quite frankly, it is far more difficult, challenging and stressful to live a life that is based on fear, doubt and guilt rather than peace, joy, love and prosperity. It is much more fun to see the good in situations and the "godness" in people than it is to see the ugliness and bad in everything and everybody. I am truly suggesting and advocating a life that is magical and mystical.

My thoughts often go back to Rudy and my moving sale. I wonder if Rudy took my words to heart or if he still hates his life, tormented by dreams he believes he can't accomplish and paralyzed because of his fear, doubt and guilt. I often pray for the Rudy's of the world. I pray that every human being finds their divine work on this planet, their fullest joy, their true love and overflowing abundance. I pray that enough people will get out of the Tribe with its scarcity thinking, its fear-based beliefs and its low self-esteem attitudes that the course of humanity can be dramatically altered. We are more than capable of changing our lives. We are truly capable of changing the world. By working with your five CEOs and filling your own life with peace, joy, love and prosperity, you are well on your way.

May you be blessed for all of your efforts. You can do it—you really can!

Your Gift is Waiting...

Did you collect your gift yet?

Please visit

www.anamazinglifenow.com

to get a special gift just for you.

*It will be very useful in helping you apply
what you have learned in this book.*

The password is the first word of Chapter 31.

Learn More About How to Become a Successful Entrepreneur.

Devil with a Briefcase – 101 Success Secrets for the Spiritual Entrepreneur

Jan's first book gives you powerful insights into how to run a business based on her more than 27 years of experience. This book delves in depth into critical business lessons she learned from her 38 years as a Jehovah's Witness. Fun, provocative and highly practical—it's been said that applying the principles in this book would change the world. It can definitely change your business!

Still Looking for Your Passion?

If you are stuck right at the beginning of the entrepreneurial journey, wondering what gifts, talents and passions you possess, check out the 2-CD set on **Finding Your Passion, Discovering the Winner, Warrior and Wizard in You.**

Are You Really an Entrepreneur?

Questioning if you have the qualities, the necessary focus and discipline, and the passion to become an entrepreneur? Those are good questions to ask BEFORE you embark on the journey. Listen to this very thought-provoking CD called: **Do You Have What it Takes to Be an Entrepreneur?**

Do you struggle with the Organization and Planning in your Business?

If you're stuck with Systems, Schedules and Business Planning, you're perfectly normal! Most entrepreneurs struggle with these areas of their business. **S.O.S. For Your Business—Systems, Organization and Structure Every Entrepreneur Needs** is all about systems, time management, setting up your business, the easiest business plan in the world that will excite you and other ways to make running your business easy and fun.

Does the Emotional Rollercoaster of Entrepreneurship have You Coming and Going?

Many entrepreneurs aren't accustomed to dealing with the ups and downs of being in business for themselves. How do you handle them easily and gracefully? What do you need as C.O.O. of your business? Who do you have to be personally in order to succeed professionally? Learn how to be outrageously successful in your business with the 2- CD set: **Who Are You? Laying the Foundation as C.O.O.** where you'll learn what it takes to be the best in your business while enjoying life!

If you hate selling the old-fashioned, pushy, put your foot in the door way, you will love **Heart to Heart Selling – Selling that Makes Everyone Feel Good**. This 2-CD set is a very different perspective on "cold-calling," objections and building relationships in business. You'll actually learn to like yourself in sales and look forward to sharing your message with others.

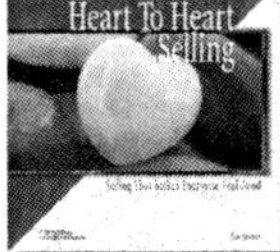

These resources and more for

Entrepreneurs are available online at:

www.janjanzen.com

Sacred Gifts

If you were fascinated about Sacred Gifts and want to know YOUR Sacred Gifts, visit www.yoursacredgifts.com   Learning about your Sacred Gifts is an awesome way to release a ton of fear, doubt and guilt!

Healing CDs

Listen in as I do live group healing sessions on various subjects such as money, weight issues and relationships. For more information on the latest offerings available, go to www.anamazinglifenow.com

Speaking Engagements

A top notch speaker who "wows" her audience, Jan Janzen is a dynamic speaker with passion, energy and wisdom to share! Her message is a combination of 'real world' knowledge, coupled with a huge desire to reach people's hearts and motivate them to long-term success. For more information on Jan as a speaker, please visit www.janjanzen.com

To have Jan Janzen appear live at your next event, please email speaker@janjanzen.com. Networking organizations, corporations, charity events, and churches are welcome to call. Opportunities to create revenue-producing events for your organization are available.

What Jan's Audience Has to Say:

"I know I already told you tonight but I just had to mention again, I was super impressed with your presence and command of the stage. I've seen a lot of top-notch speakers and boy, you've got what it takes! Put your seat belt on 'cause you're going far. Awesome."

–Kim Baker, Vancouver, B.C.

"Jan Janzen is one of the most dynamic and powerful speakers I have heard. She is transparent, honest and funny! She is real! She is a dynamo. She is gifted in her ability to communicate timeless truths with love. You will be transformed when you hear Jan speak."

–Andrea Scott, Toronto, Ontario

"All I can say is that not only do I admire you and your strength. I admire how in one night I was truly pumped up. You did that, in your total belief that we can all reach our goals and assisting each other to greatness is the way to go."

–Caroline Loach, Personal Coach

About the Author...

Jan Janzen

I spent the first 38 years of my life as a Jehovah's Witness. Leaving the religious organization in 1999 set me on a path of deep spiritual and personal discovery. Today, I am an ordained nondenominational minister and have redefined for myself a spirituality that works in real life.

I bought my first franchise at the age of 19 and have been an entrepreneur for more than 27 years. My first book, **Devil with a Briefcase, 101 Success Secrets for the Spiritual Entrepreneur** along with my Spiritual Entrepreneur CD series have helped guide entrepreneurs who want it all—fun, values and profit in their businesses *while* making a difference in the world.

Over the last few years, it has been an honor and a pleasure to work with clients from all over the world. Using my Sacred Gift of Healing to help them find their power, purpose and abundance while feeling more peaceful than they ever thought possible is a joy beyond compare.

Today, I am the President of Plexus Pink, a network marketing company that is committed to breast health for every woman on the planet. It is an exciting journey to bring spiritual principles that work in a very practical way to a global network of Ambassadors.

It's certainly been a·fascinating balance to juggle a full-time career with client work and writing, speaking and teaching while finding time for the people who are important in my life—including me! To date, I am thrilled with the results of the balancing act.

I am blessed to spend most of the year in Mexico, where I get to live a truly magical life that is abundant in love, joy, peace and prosperity, the very foundation of my work.

                      www.janjanzen.com